3

D0296642

FROM LAST TO FIRST

A long-distance runner's journey
from failure to success

Charlie Spedding

Published in Great Britain
2011 by Aurum Press Ltd
7 Greenland Street
London NW1 0ND
www.aurumpress.co.uk

All photographs courtesy of Charlie Spedding

ISBN 978 1 84513 628 4

1 3 5 7 9 10 8 6 4 2
2011 2013 2015 2014 2012

CONTENTS

INTRODUCTION

Talent is the key to high performance, or so you might think. I won a Bronze medal in the Olympic marathon, but I was definitely not one of the three most talented distance runners in the world. I was a talented runner compared to the average runner, but you don't run against average runners in an Olympic final. Among that elite group of people I was not particularly talented. So how did I win a medal?

Most people believe our level of performance should be the same as our level of talent, assuming we have trained properly for our event. But have you ever had a bad day, a really bad day when you performed well below your level of talent? That straight line between talent and performance can be bent downwards by circumstances.

I believe that if you can bend it down on a bad day, you can also bend it up. I believe that on occasions you can create the circumstances in which you can perform at a higher level than your talent says you can. This is one of the beauties of sport. This is what makes the outcome of every event uncertain. This is what gives the underdog his hopes and dreams. This is why sport brings passion and excitement to our lives.

This book has taken a couple of decades to write. I have written it in the little bits of spare time I could find in the life of a husband and father, and the demands of work and running a business. I have written it for three reasons. Firstly, for the same reason I ran; to see if I could do it and try to reach that goal no matter how long it took. Secondly, I hope there is someone who may read something in my story which helps them in the same way that I improved, thanks to the help and advice of others. Last, but not least, I have enjoyed writing it; and I hope that somebody somewhere enjoys reading it.

The structure of this book has hardly changed from the first draft I wrote, but there have been many refinements to that original text. I would like to thank the people who helped me to make those changes and bring this project to its conclusion.

David Huntley, my brother-in-law, read the first draft. Thanks to his input I produced a second version, which I showed to Tom Knight, former Athletics correspondent of the *Daily Telegraph* and John Bryant, author of several books including *The Marathon Makers*. Both Tom and John helped me, not only with their experience, but also their encouragement and enthusiasm.

Last, but certainly not least, I thank my wife, Christina, who worked tirelessly as my editor. If you discover a split infinitive, please don't tell her.

Chapter 1

LOS ANGELES

As I walked from the bus to the gymnasium at the Santa Monica College Stadium, I saw the white Olympic flag with its five coloured rings hanging limply in the hot sunshine. The temperature inside the gym was much lower than outside, but the cooler air was filled with simmering anxiety as 107 nervous men checked in for the Los Angeles Olympic Marathon.

I sat on the floor to pin number 396 to my British running vest, and I watched Boston marathon winner and American record holder, Alberto Salazar, stretching. Next to him former Olympic medallist Rod Dixon of New Zealand was chatting to my British team-mate Geoff Smith. Geoff had run the fastest time by a Briton for several years when he finished second to Rod in New York. Juma Ikanga and Gidamis Shahanga, silver and gold medallists from the Commonwealth Games, were jogging slowly around the room. Toshihiko Seko, who had been undefeated at the marathon for five years, listened intently to his coach, along with his Japanese teammates. Everyone else either stared at the floor or gazed at Carlos Lopes, the Portuguese double World Cross Country Champion, and Rob de Castella, the reigning World Marathon Champion.

The media experts had all proclaimed this to be the best marathon field ever assembled; but as they eagerly awaited the race, some of the runners were suffering torment during the final hour of waiting. They were filling up with awe for the occasion and the opposition, and with fear for the distance and heat they were about to endure. Some stared blankly into the distance, while others talked incessantly about their training, races and injuries. Some were motionless but others jogged and moved continually. The room was shaded and cool, but the air was charged as if a thunderstorm was about to erupt.

My anxiety level was increasing rapidly as the ultimate challenge of an Olympic marathon came closer and closer. My mind was racing and my stomach was churning. I was on the verge of losing control. I needed to get back in control, and quickly. I walked outside onto the track where the race would start. The heat from the August sunshine was intense, and it didn't make sense to stay there long, but I had to compose myself, which is something I do best when I am alone. Nobody else was crazy enough to stand out in the sunshine, so I had the solitude I needed.

I took some deep breaths and started talking to myself. When I was inside the gym I was looking at all those great runners and thinking, 'How am I going to beat him and him and him?' But now that I was outside and alone I started to think differently, 'I have prepared for this race as well as I can. Today is the day. This is the biggest race of my life and I believe I am ready to run the greatest race of my life. Nobody else can stop me from running my greatest race, and if I do it, I am going to beat a lot of them.' I started to feel in control, and with that feeling came more confidence, and on top of that came some inspiration. 'I know I am going to run better than ever, and because I have never done that before I don't know how good it could be. All the best runners are here today, which means that with one brilliant performance I could beat all the greatest marathon runners in the world. I just need to do it once in my life to beat them all. All these guys being here isn't a problem, it's an opportunity. A fantastic, wonderful opportunity!'

By changing the situation from a problem to an opportunity, I changed my frame of mind from confused to focused and positive. When I walked back into the relative cool of the gymnasium I looked at Lopes, de Castella, Salazar, Seko and all the others, and I realised that this was indeed the precise moment for me to produce the performance of my life. I still felt extremely nervous, but I was no longer scared. I just wanted to get on with it.

When it was time to go back out into the sunshine and heat, I jogged a lap of the track with a very positive frame of mind. After a long drink of water, I ran a few gentle strides and tried to ignore my churning stomach. As we were called to the starting line I tipped two cups of water over my head to soak my hair and shoulders. With cold water dripping down my back I lined up in the third row beside John Treacy, who, like Lopes, had been the World Cross Country Champion twice.

The race started with two and three-quarter laps of the track, which was very crowded on the bends in the middle of a bunch of 107 runners. The running was a little more relaxed on the road outside the stadium, but the tension remained high as the crowds along both sides of the road bombarded us with noise. I have never known such excitement at a road race; the Angelinos were proud of hosting the Olympics and they were excited about the marathon.

The first few miles were a little uncomfortable as I tried to settle into a rhythm and adjust my bodily systems to running 26.2 miles in 85 to 90 degrees of heat. I was content to run in the midst of the group, and just get a few miles behind me. I started to feel better, as if things were in equilibrium, by about four miles, just as we turned onto San Vicente Boulevard. This was one of the most crowded sections of the course, and the noise was deafening. By chance, I found myself running beside the media's pre-race favourite and World Champion, Rob de Castella. For some reason I decided to show him how relaxed I was, as if he cared, by having a chat with him.

I said, 'Noisy, isn't it?' to which he replied, 'What?' which rather proved my point. And that, verbatim, is the entire extent of the conversations I had during the whole race.

The Dutchman and European Champion, Gerard Nijboer, had tried some early pace setting, but now abandoned it for an easier ride in the pack. I had slowly moved closer to the front and we were all running slightly downhill towards the Pacific Ocean in a large, tightly grouped bunch as we passed 10 kilometres in 31 minutes and 15 seconds, which is even paced schedule for a finishing time of 2 hours 11 minutes and 40 seconds. This was good steady running, but not spectacular, which was exactly what I was hoping for on such a hot day. I was concentrating on staying relaxed, running efficiently and finding whatever shade there was from the direct glare of the sun. My plan was to get as far into the race as possible for the least amount of energy expenditure, in the hope that I would have something left for the closing stages.

It was all going just the way I wanted until we turned on to Ocean Drive and Ahmed Ismail of Somalia forged ahead, running the seventh mile in 4 minutes 45 seconds. I decided to be smart, and just let him go. Running so fast so soon in this heat had to be crazy, and I was sure he couldn't possibly keep it up. A group of other African runners, who all loved to run at the front, thought otherwise, and decided to follow him. Ikangaa was one of those runners, and as soon as de Castella realised that Ikangaa was pulling away, he neatly stepped out of the pack and gave chase.

The race was suddenly changing and I had to make a decision. Should I continue with my sensible even pace, or should I get up to the front? I really had no choice. An hour earlier I had told myself that if I ran the greatest race of my life, I could fulfil my wildest dreams. I couldn't possibly let such a talented group get away. I had to abandon caution and seize my opportunity. I accelerated and worked my way back towards the leaders.

I was six seconds behind Ismail and Ikangaa at 15 km, with a time of 46:06. I had covered the previous 5 km in a dangerously fast 14 minutes 51 seconds, but I was on the back of the leading group, and everyone behind me was effectively out of the race from that point on. Geoff Smith and Alberto Salazar either didn't or couldn't go with that surge, and their Olympic dreams were already over. We had just turned onto Pacific Boulevard when we passed 10 miles in 49:35, and from here the course was either flat or uphill all the way to the Coliseum.

Somalia's moment of Olympic glory came to an end as Ismail faded from the scene, and drifted back to finish 47th. The pace setting was taken up briefly by Nijboer, and then by Joseph Nzau of Kenya. I was content again to maintain my position and concentrate on picking the shortest route. Nobody seemed keen to commit himself, so the pace slackened slightly and a dozen of us formed a tightly knit group.

We passed 20 km in 61:26, having run 30:11 for the second 10 km. We reached half way in just under 65 minutes, with Ikangaa and Nzau in the lead, and I ran just behind them. I was feeling comfortable. (Comfortable is a relative term of course: I was comfortable compared to how I might have felt at this stage of a marathon, run in 85 degrees.) I knew I was running really well. I felt strong, and in control. I had beaten Ikangaa in the London Marathon and I felt I could do it again. Now that we had passed half way my confidence was growing, and I started to look around. Carlos Lopes was running beside me, but I had to look again to believe what I was seeing. We were travelling at about 12 miles per hour, with 14 miles behind us, but Lopes looked smooth and totally effortless. He even appeared to be running with his mouth closed, finding it sufficient to breathe through his nose. I felt comfortable, but Lopes appeared to be jogging.

In what I can only assume was an attempt to cause some excitement, Rod Dixon appeared at the front with an injection of pace. It was a futile attempt, which only lasted quarter of a mile, before he faded and drifted away from the leading pack. It was becoming apparent that the real race wouldn't start for another five or six miles, and anyone with serious intentions was biding his time. Nobody wanted to sacrifice himself by leading for too long, in such hot conditions, with such a talented group on his heels.

From 15 to 18 miles we ran in a strange and unaccustomed silence because the route went up onto the Marina Freeway, which was an elevated motorway from which spectators were banned. It was an ugly expanse of hot concrete, normally crowded with cars and trucks, but which I shared with a small group of skinny men from the four corners of the world. There were three Japanese, Toshihiko Seko and the Soh twins, Takeshi and Shigeru; two Djiboutians, Jama Robleh and Ahmed Salah; an Irishman, John Treacy; an Australian, Rob de Castella; a Kenyan, Joe Nzau; a Tanzanian, Juma Ikangaa; and the man from Portugal, Carlos Lopes.

As we left the freeway and were greeted again with tumultuous applause, I realised quite clearly that with this cosmopolitan group, I shared not only the road, but also the experience of a lifetime. I was struck with a sudden awareness of who I was and where I was: a 32 year old second son of a County Durham chemist, a runner with 16 years training and two failed attempts to make previous Olympic teams behind me. I had been a complete outsider to make this team before the trial, but was now leading the Olympic marathon at 18 miles, feeling good, and knowing that whatever the final outcome, I was racing with the best in the world, and on this most important day, I was one of them. I could not resist the opportunity to grin and wave back at the crowd. I felt absolutely wonderful.

In this almost euphoric state I passed 30 km in 1:33:02, and perhaps I was feeling comfortable because the pace had slowed to 31:36 for the last 10 km. My elation did not last much longer, as I realised that the moment of truth was soon to arrive. I began to prepare my mind for the inevitable lung-bursting, gut-wrenching, eye-popping surge of pace that would carry someone to victory. I expected Rob de Castella to make just such a move close to the 20 miles point, but we passed that landmark without incident in 1:39:52.

After feeling so relaxed a little earlier, my mind was frantic now. I was continually talking to myself, 'Come on; make your move. As soon as you come past I'm going with you. Let's go. I'm ready.' I glanced around and to my surprise realised that de Castella, the reigning Commonwealth and World Champion, was right at the back of the group, and quite clearly, he was not about to take this race by the scruff of the neck and sort it out.

I looked around at the rest of the leading group, and tried to pick the one most likely to take the initiative. With rising anxiety, I realised that apart from Ikangaa, who was already leading, every single one of them was probably quite happy to run in a bunch all the way to the stadium and take their chances in a sprint for the finish. Seko would be delighted with that situation, but it would be no use to me. I had ended up running marathons because I had never been able to out sprint anybody.

Everyday for weeks beforehand, I had spent hours mentally rehearsing this race. I planned my reactions to a host of possibilities, and I thought I had covered every conceivable situation. I had prepared myself physically and mentally for a long, hard effort over the last six miles, and I knew this was my best chance in a field with so many fast finishers. But I now realised that I was faced with a situation I had completely overlooked, because in all my planning it had never once occurred to me that I would get to 21 miles in the Olympic marathon and feel that the pace was too slow! I realised that I was going to have to take the initiative and break the group apart. All my preparation and rehearsal had convinced me that I would run beyond my previous best, but I was running so well I was faced with a situation I had never foreseen. For the second time in the race I had to make a crucial decision.

It took me half a mile or so to adjust my mind to the reality of what I knew I had to do, and while I was preparing myself for a surge that would have to last for nearly half an hour, we passed a drinks station. Everyone veered off to the right-hand side of the road, inevitably slowing down and bumping into each other, as they tried to grab their personalised water bottles. I did not feel the need for more liquid as strongly as my desire to shake up the race, so I ran straight on, and immediately found myself a few yards clear. I made the most of this by increasing the pace slightly, which meant the others had to work hard to catch me.

Ikangaa quickly resumed the role of leader, but we were travelling a little faster now, and I stayed very close to his shoulder to keep the pressure on. The group was slightly smaller, and a quick glance confirmed that de Castella was dropped. It may be the oldest trick in the book, but accelerating past a water station still works.

The World Champion had been dropped with a slight

increase in pace, and his departure was a timely reminder that reputations count for nothing in the heat of competition. My focus, determination and concentration were now total. After sixteen years and thousands and thousands of miles of training, I had reached the defining moment of my whole career. I moved past Ikangaa and into the lead. I cranked up the pace until I was running as fast as I dared. I wanted my action to be decisive, but not suicidal. I knew I had to hold it for another five miles. Having committed myself, and everyone else, to a long, hard finish, there could be no thoughts of changing my mind.

I took the pace from 5 minutes per mile up to 4 minutes 47 seconds, and suddenly it was hurting. After so many miles of waiting for the attack to come, it was a magnificent feeling to be the one attacking. I didn't need to look round to see what was happening because the sun was low in the sky and directly behind us. I couldn't see the other runners but I could see their shadows on the road in front of me. I pushed on and on, and as each hard-earned quarter mile went by, another shadow disappeared.

I ran like this for a mile and a half, with aching tiredness building in my legs, but with my mind focused deeply on the job of putting one foot in front of the other as smoothly, efficiently and quickly as I could. My concentration was intense; I could have run straight through the wildest Hollywood scenes and never have noticed. It was as if my 16 years of training were all distilled into this brief moment.

The spell was finally broken by mounting discomfort, and my desire to see who was still with me. A quick peep behind revealed that Lopes, Treacy and Nzau remained. It wasn't just who was there, as how many, that worried me. They say that fourth is the worst place to finish in the Olympics, and I certainly didn't want to lead these three to the medals and be left with nothing for myself. Having done my fair share of the work, I decided to drop in behind Lopes and Treacy. I hoped that by following for a while I could compose myself for another attack later on.

Lopes, however, had other ideas. Having just settled in behind him, we passed the 23 mile mark, and he took this as his cue to say goodbye. He simply changed gears and surged away. I instinctively went after him, trying to run in his slipstream with my eyes fixed on his back. Treacy was directly behind me, trying desperately to hang on, but this 36 year old Portuguese was in the process of running the next mile in a mere 4 minutes and 38 seconds. After 200 yards I felt I was on the verge of sprinting, and with 5 kilometres still to run, I had to give way. As I returned to my previous pace John Treacy came alongside me, but he could not get past. Lopes steadily pulled away and with him went any chance of the gold medal.

Just as I was accepting the inevitable departure of Lopes, I suddenly realised that Nzau was nowhere to be seen. 'I am going to win a medal,' flashed across my brain. My wildest dream, my lifelong ambition was about to come true, if of course, and only if, I could keep going for another three miles. John and I never spoke to each other during those weary miles on Exposition Drive, but we both knew that by running together we stood a better chance of keeping our positions. We each tried to pull away from the other on a couple of occasions, but our efforts were made to maintain our speed as much as to break away. We were running at 4 minutes 50 seconds per mile, and it was hurting. My whole body ached, and my legs were stinging. The crowds may still have been shouting, but it no longer felt like a great occasion - this was pain, and I wanted it to be over.

We pressed on along this endless road, and somewhere near 25 miles the shadow of a head suddenly appeared at our feet. In horror we both looked round, but there was no runner to be seen. The head belonged to the driver of a television motorbike,

10

which had crept up behind us. Our relief was fleeting, because the continuous fear of being caught drove us on.

At last we reached the approach to the Coliseum, and I started to think in terms of the silver medal instead of just a medal. There was a right angle turn onto the Stadium approach road, and I attacked this bend and surged out of the other side, but Treacy was right beside me. I decided to try again at the sharp corner that led down to the tunnel and through the stands. I was busy thinking about my next move when Treacy made his, and he caught me out. 100 yards before the turn he surged away and quickly had eight yards on me. I had to catch him before we reached the track or it would be too late. I accelerated hard but was only holding him. I hurtled down the ramp but he still had eight yards. I had to close the gap, and hammered through the tunnel as hard as I could. As we emerged from the tunnel onto the running track I was right behind him, but my legs and lungs were exploding.

With a lap and a quarter of the track to run, I fixed my eyes on his green vest and tried to glue myself to him. We seemed to be running faster and faster, and with 350 yards to go, a gap started to open. Along the back straight he stretched his lead to eight yards again. Try as I did, my legs just wouldn't go any faster. Around the final bend my body was screaming for rest, but as I hit the home straight I found one more effort, but all I could do was hold him.

Treacy crossed the line in 2:09:56, and I was there two seconds later. Lopes had won in a new Olympic record of 2:09:21, having run the stretch from 35 to 40 km in 14:33. Treacy and I had gone under 30 minutes for the last 10 km, and he had shaken me off with a final 400 meters in 67 seconds. The fourth man, Takeshi Soh, was a minute behind me, de Castella came fifth and Ikangaa finished sixth.

When I finally got my hands off my knees and my

breathing back to normal, I took a drink of water and looked around at the Olympic Stadium. I was stunned and emotionless. I felt as if the race had used up all my determination, then my will power and then my emotions. I wandered around the infield in a daze; unable to react to everything that had happened. John Treacy was waving to his family in the stands. I walked over to him. We still didn't speak, but we exchanged a look of respect, a grin and then a hug.

CHAPTER 2

LOS ANGELES REACTION

The morning after the race I woke at about 5:30am. My body was tired but my mind couldn't rest. I got up and walked, slowly, around the deserted Olympic village, and then out on to the street. This was the first time I had been alone since attempting to calm my nerves before the race started. My legs were stiff and sore, which was inevitable after running twenty-six miles, and I didn't mind the soreness, because I expected it. However, I had not expected to feel the way I did mentally. I was still feeling numb, as if all the emotion had been sucked out of me. I felt happy, but I had a strange feeling that something was out of place.

After wandering around aimlessly for a while, I bought a newspaper, and read how three European runners had confounded the experts with a clean sweep of the marathon medals. With only three previous marathons between them, a Portuguese, an Irishman and an Englishman had overcome the heat, and their more experienced opponents, in a thrilling climax to the Olympic Games. I felt as if I was reading about the sort of people I had marvelled at for years; the sort of people who I had always believed were somehow different to ordinary mortals. When I read my name among them, I realised what was out of place. I had always assumed that ordinary people like me didn't win Olympic medals. If it was such a great achievement, how come I had done it? I had been able to produce a supreme effort because the Olympics were so important to me, but I had always held it in such high esteem that my new status was very hard to come to terms with. Would I have to change, or was it just the image I had of myself that would have to change?

When I got home I realised that I was still the same, but other people thought I was different. I was in demand, and a lot of people wanted some of my time. My success in Los Angeles coincided with the running boom. The London Marathon and Great North Run had both started three years earlier, and thousands of people who had never run before were attempting half marathons and full marathons. They were all full of enthusiasm, but short of knowledge, so a lot of the races held seminars and invited people like me to talk to the runners.

I spent a lot of time travelling the country to attend these events. Some of them were big occasions and some were small. One of the largest groups I spoke to was in Lincoln when I addressed 500 runners the night before the Lincoln Half Marathon. Even at the time, I thought the night before was a little late to be advising them on their training, but that's what I did.

Not all of the seminars were held in conjunction with a race. The best time to be informed and motivated is well before the targeted race. The middle of winter, when training can be difficult, seemed like an ideal time to pass on useful information to eager runners, so I agreed to be part of a mid-winter seminar in Barrow-in-Furness. If you have ever driven to Barrow you will realise that wherever you set off from, it is a difficult place to get to. I was living in Durham at the time and had to cross the Pennines and then the Lake District. It was either sleeting or snowing the entire way there. I was delayed by road works, accidents, floods, broken down tractors and diversions. It took hours and hours to get there. Luckily, I had given myself plenty of time, and arrived just before the seminar started. I was one of a panel of experts; there was a coach, a podiatrist, a dietician, and two runners. There were five of us on the panel, which was one more than there was in the audience.

No matter how many people came to the seminar I was always asked a lot of questions. Everybody wanted to know about training, shoes and diet, though once I was asked what I thought about breathing. I replied that I wholeheartedly recommended it. A big concern was always diet; so much so that I think a lot of newcomers to running were hoping they would be able to eat themselves into peak physical condition, rather than follow my advice, which involved quite a lot of training. There were various fad foods, supplements and diets, and I was often asked if eating this or that would improve performance. Once I was asked about cottage cheese, and I told them never to eat cottage cheese because it is the most fattening food in the world. I explained that I didn't have any scientific evidence for this, but I have been all over the world and I have never seen anybody except fat people eat that stuff.

I had done a couple of seminars before the Games, but at every seminar afterwards I was asked the inevitable question, 'How does it feel to win an Olympic medal?' When people asked me this they were genuinely interested, but they always gave the impression they already knew the answer. After all, they had watched the Games on television, and from the comfort of their armchairs they had been able to experience the ecstasy of victory and the agony of defeat as it happened, and then again in slow motion.

The typical image of Olympic success comes from watching the 100 meters final. The athletes nervously go to their blocks; the starter's commands ring out in a hushed stadium;

eight strong men suddenly launch into action; they sprint flat out along the track and flash across the line. In that final moment, and only then, does the winner realise he has won. Accompanied by the other medallists, he immediately starts to dance up and down, slapping his hands, and waving his arms in the air. The sheer joy of this supreme victory flows out of him in a cascading display of pure happiness and ecstatic bliss.

I had to tell them that it isn't quite like that in the marathon. When Carlos Lopes pulled away, and John Treacy and I moved clear of Joe Nzau at 23 miles, I knew I was going to win a medal. I clearly remember that wonderful moment of realisation. However, I couldn't start jumping up and down and waving my arms in the air because I still had three miles to run. I provisionally had an Olympic medal, and it would be mine as long as I could keep going for the next fifteen minutes. As I ran those last miles and my tiredness increased, I had to channel all the excitement back into my running, and use my emotion to put one foot in front of the other. When I finally reached the stadium and crossed the line, and the medal was definitely mine, I did not jump up and down or wave my arms in the air, because the only thing I felt was relief; relief that I had not lost it.

'Okay,' they said to me, 'the marathon is a weird event, and it's not like the others. But it must be a wonderful experience to come through the tunnel into a spectacular Olympic stadium after all those miles of road, and run the final lap in front of such a huge, cheering crowd. The marathon is so special because of that finish in the stadium.'

I suppose it normally is, but as I ran the final lap around the Coliseum, the only thing I saw was a green and white vest of Ireland, with two scrawny, pale arms sticking out of it, slowly edging away from me. It wasn't until after I crossed the line, that I became aware of the magnificent surroundings. Only then did I see the crowd, only then did I hear the noise, and only then did

I appreciate the Olympic stage upon which I had been running. I had finished third, despite my last lap battle, so I might as well have been 100 yards behind, but safely ahead of fourth. Then I could have appreciated the last lap, and enjoyed the occasion, but my lasting memory of that moment will always be John Treacy's back.

'Okay, okay,' they continue, 'Your circumstances were unusual, but you must have enjoyed the closing ceremonies. The marathon finished as the closing ceremony began - it was an integral part of the whole spectacular finish. I saw those fireworks on television, and they were brilliant. It must have been wonderful to be right in the middle of that enormous party, having just run the race of your life.'

The medal presentation was a fantastic experience for me. As trumpets heralded the medalists approach, Lopes, Treacy and I walked across the track in line and then up onto a huge stage in the middle of the arena. I was stiff-legged but not as bad as Treacy, who needed a push from me to get up the steps. We stood behind the rostrum, and as a hush fell over the stadium, a Geordie voice from behind me shouted, 'Well done, Charlie.' I looked around to see who it was, which was pointless, because 40,000 faces were looking back at me. After Juan Antonio Samaranch, the President of the International Olympic Committee, had hung the medal around my neck, I proudly watched the Union Jack climb the smallest of three flagpoles whilst struggling to sing along to the Portuguese national anthem.

The closing ceremony party began as our presentation finished. However, from the moment I had crossed the finishing line I had been accompanied by an Olympic official, who had made sure that I did not take any drinks or food from anyone but himself. As I left the presentation podium, he escorted me through a tunnel underneath the stands, and out of the stadium to a port-a-cabin in the corner of the car park. Th ere I was subjected to my first drug test.

It is a terrible indictment of modern sport that such things should be necessary, but unfortunately they are, and I was always happy to co-operate. Th e tests, I hoped, would catch the offenders, resulting in their disqualification, and would also prove that I was always clean. Th e procedure was straightforward; a urine sample was all that was required. After answering a few questions and signing a declaration, I was given a plastic beaker and, accompanied by my designated official, I retired to a cubicle in the corner of this caravan in the car park of the Coliseum.

Can you imagine how hard it is to produce urine into a plastic beaker, after running twenty six miles as hard as you can in 85 degrees of heat, with a complete stranger staring at you? Well, that is where I spent the whole of the closing ceremony.

No matter how poorly my experiences fit the expectations of others, I was always happy to talk to people about them, and especially about the thrill of competing at the highest level. It was my constant hope that among all the people I came across, I might really, truly reach somebody. Perhaps there was one young runner in all those audiences who would be inspired by what I said. Perhaps, like me, he would be engulfed with the vision and desire to be his very best, and after many years of hard training and commitment he would make it to the British team. Maybe, then, he would travel to some distant city where he would perform with fearless conviction, and superlative effort. Then, in the shadow of that famous five ringed flag maybe, just maybe, he too could stand with pride in a port-a-cabin with a plastic beaker in his hand.

My speaking engagements soon diversified from runners' seminars to fund raising dinners and sports club award nights. After a few more months, I was receiving invitations from groups with no connections to sport at all. The most unusual one I ever received was from a local institution in Sedgefield. There was a hospital there called Winterton Psychiatric Hospital, and a new consultant psychiatrist had recently been appointed. He believed that some of his patients were not mentally ill but merely eccentric. Their eccentricity had made them feel like outcasts in their communities, which had led some of them to depression. He felt that if they could accept their eccentricity and learn to feel all right about it they could return to living at home. Part of his plan was to introduce them to a variety of people who were very much accepted in life, but did slightly eccentric things. He considered that running 26 miles 385 yards as fast as possible, qualified me to speak to these people.

This was such a strange invitation that I accepted it. After all, I was living a happy and healthy life, and it would be good for my soul to give something back to society and those less fortunate than me. On the day of the talk I arrived early and was met in the car park by the consultant. As we had plenty of time he showed me some of the occupational therapy workshops they used, and explained how important it was to keep the patients active in both body and mind. In the last room one of the patients was finishing some work.

The consultant whispered to me, 'That's Tom. He's been here a long time, but he has made a lot of progress. I will introduce you to him.'

We walked over and the consultant said, 'Charlie, this is Tom. Tom, this is Charlie Spedding. He is an Olympic bronze medallist in the marathon.'

Tom looked at me, and then with a gentle smile he put one hand on my shoulder. He leaned slightly towards me, and in a soft, comforting voice he said, 'Charlie, it's alright. When I came in here I thought I was Henry the Eighth.'

CHAPTER 3

EARLY DAYS

I was born in 1952, when my parents lived in Ferryhill, County Durham. Local legend says that it is so named because it is the hill on which Roger de Fery killed a fierce wild boar, which had been terrorising the neighbourhood in the twelfth century, and that Roger was a descendent of one of the French Barons who came over to England with William the Conqueror. Nothing more was written about Ferryhill until the 1960s when a prominent architect completed a comprehensive survey and decreed that Ferryhill was the ugliest town in the North of England. Of course, there have been many changes to the place since then, and as far as I can tell, the local planners have done everything in their power to ensure the town maintains its status.

In the centre of town there is a large rectangular open space, which used to be the village green. The Town Hall overlooks it from the east. Old, stone built shops and pubs line the south side, and there is still a farm on the north side. Unfortunately the green itself is now a bus station and car park, but that's progress. Ferryhill, like many other places, was transformed from an agricultural village to an industrial town by the discovery of coal, and the building of row upon row of terraced houses for the miners.

We lived in Main Street, just along the road from the bus station. I shared a bedroom at the back of the house with my brother Michael, who is three years older. From the bedroom window we had a panoramic view across our back garden to the chimney, winding gear and slagheap of the colliery. The pit closed many years ago and the slagheap has been grassed over; landscaped would be an exaggeration. The noise and dirt have gone now, but so have most of the jobs.

My father, Joe, was a pharmacist and he owned the chemist shop in Main Street. We lived above the shop, which was very convenient for my dad going to work, but very inconvenient when people ran out of aspirin, baby food or corn plasters on Sunday morning. He was born during the First World War, so he was in his twenties during the Second World War. He spent most of the war as the pharmacist in a field hospital in Egypt, and he always said he was very lucky to have never faced any bullets. His elder brother, George, was a rear gunner in a Lancaster bomber, and he was very lucky as well; he lived.

At the end of the war my father and mother, Mabel, were married. He started working as a relief manager for a company with a chain of chemist shops. However, instead of saving money for his married life, he was obliged to spend the first few years paying off the debts his father had amassed, but was unable to honour. Having done his duty for his country, he then had to do his duty for his family, and for the rest of his life he hated the idea of being in debt. But, of course, that is exactly where he found himself in 1950 when he bought the business in Ferryhill. My parents had done without any luxuries during the war, they had done without any luxuries while my grandfather's debts were paid, and they decided to do without any again until the loan on the business was cleared. They paid off a ten-year mortgage in three and a half years, and then had what they wanted; a business of their own, and indebted to no-one. I should probably add that my father always credited the flu epidemic of 1951-52, with his ability to repay his debts early, rather than just his frugal life-style.

I was completely unaware of all this as I languished near the bottom of Mr Ford's class at Dean Bank Junior School. I was usually either fortieth or forty-first in a class of 42, so I feel justified in saying I was near the bottom. My excuse has always been that I had an operation to correct a squint in my left eye at three years old, and I had to wear a patch over my right eye to make the weaker, left eye work. I assume that because of this I learnt to read later than the other children, although my mother removed the patch earlier than she was supposed to because I kept crashing into the furniture. This has always been my excuse, but the truth is probably that I had far more interest in playing outside than doing schoolwork.

Unfortunately, playing outside at school usually involved ball games, and despite always wanting to take part, my eyesight kept my performance at a similar level to my grades in the classroom. With my glasses off I would see double, and when two balls were coming towards me I only had a 50-50 chance of catching or kicking the right one. Sometimes it was very embarrassing when I swung my leg at a football and missed completely.

Then, one sunny summer day, we all trooped along the road to Dean Bank Recreation Ground for my first experience of Sports Day. The only event was the 100 yards sprint, but Mr Ford very thoughtfully handicapped the races on height. He assumed that bigger boys could run faster than smaller boys. I was the shortest in my heat, and received the biggest start. The other five boys were from one to five yards behind me. I thought this was fantastic. I loved running about in the sunshine, and I only had to run from here to there. I had a start on everybody else and I felt sure I was going to win.

The race began. I sprinted hard. After twenty yards I was second; by fifty yards I was third; at the finish I was last.

I still remember that race vividly. I was devastated. How could this happen? How could I lose after being given a start? Why could I not run as fast as other boys? How come I was no good at anything? Running was of no interest to me at all after that experience, but I was interested in football, and I spent a lot of time kicking a football against our back wall. I used to pass the ball to myself off the wall and then turn and shoot, with the garage doors as my goal. As far as I remember I won six or seven FA Cup Finals single-handedly with a hat trick in each game, or perhaps even in each half. Whichever it was, I spent hours and hours running about, and it must have given me some basic fitness and stamina.

My next school was the Chorister School in Durham; I was at the school, but not in the choir, as singing is something else I cannot do. I continued my enjoyment of football by playing in the school yard every break time, and often after school as well. One of the lads I played with was a boy called Tony Blair. I don't recall his skill with the ball, but I do remember his ability to make up rules of the game to suit his team's situation. Once, when a team mate of mine fell over, but still managed to kick the tennis ball against the wall, between the two pullovers, Tony managed to convince all of his team, and some of mine, that it was against the rules to kick the ball when you were on the ground. I should have realised that he was destined for a life in politics.

My next experience of running was at this school, but this time we had a cross country race. Purists would not describe the riverbank footpaths of Durham as cross country, but importantly this race was longer, considerably longer, than the 100 yards of my previous event. I was determined not to come last, and I was prepared to run as hard as I could to avoid a repeat dose of utter humiliation.

I was determined but I was also probably quite naïve, because most of the boys didn't care where they finished, and only ran until they were out of sight of the teacher. Obviously they didn't suffer, as I did, from the demons of previous failure. I ran hard and was quickly with a small leading bunch. A steep hill sorted us all out and I pressed on to finish second. I was thrilled because I had found something I could do better than most people, rather than my usual experience of doing everything worse than most people. At the time I knew nothing at all about needing fast-twitch muscle fibres to sprint and slow-twitch muscle fibres for stamina. A physiologist would have realised from my experiences that I had a very low percentage of fast-twitch fibres and high percentage of slow-twitch fibres. I was never going to be able to sprint fast, but ask me to keep going and I had the right kind of legs to do it. Unfortunately, my school didn't employ a physiologist to analyse the results of the fourth form cross-country, so I was left to figure out for myself that I could be successful at running simply by trying hard. I didn't need team mates or 20-20 vision; I just had to try hard. After being so consistently devoid of success in everything else, I was very happy to make the effort to find success in something.

The boy who beat me in that first cross country race was called Dennis McConkey, and he could beat me any time he had a mind to. He clearly had some running ability, but he didn't have the inclination to try in every race; so throughout my time at that school I either won or came second to Dennis. We only ran occasionally because the main sports were cricket and rugby. This was a shame because I was still just as keen to play football, and would do so with a tennis ball every lunch break. Running was never going to be everybody's favourite activity, but my consistent success gave me some sort of status in the school, which was fantastic for the boy wearing glasses at the bottom of the class.

I seem to be a slow starter at most things, but by the time I moved to Durham School, aged 13, my academic work was improving. After Mr Ford's class there was really only one way it could go. During the first term, I hauled myself up to the middle of the class, and played for the school rugby team. Cross country took place during the first half of the Easter term, and with no Dennis McConkey, I won the trial for the school junior team. Our first race was against Barnard Castle, and I soon discovered they had two good runners. By halfway, the three of us were clear of the rest. On a winding narrow path through the woods, I was in third place and feeling very tired. I felt sure I couldn't hold on much longer, but I didn't want to be beaten by two of them. I made up my mind to beat at least one of them, and made an extra effort on the tarmac path as we came out of the woods. I moved into second and the boy I had just passed drifted back. I had never been in such a tight competitive race. Whenever I had been this tired before I had been well clear, and I had known I was going to win. I was running really hard, but I was shoulder to shoulder with a boy from another school. Despite my tiredness I wanted to win and remembered how I had passed the other boy leaving the woods. With less than a mile to run I made another big effort, and started to move ahead.

I went on to win the race, but more importantly I learnt that it is possible to win even when you think you are going to lose. I realised that sometimes it is possible to avoid defeat as long as you refuse to accept it. Half way through the race I thought I was beaten. I was very tired and struggling to keep up, but from somewhere within me came the determination to keep trying. At that stage I didn't think I could win, but giving up and settling for third was an option I never contemplated.

This race was a significant event for me, because it was my first really competitive encounter. I don't know why or how I was tough enough to win, but I often wonder if my father's influence was helping me. Dad never sat me down and gave me the 'if you want to be successful in life you have to be like me, son' lecture, but his determination, attitudes and never-give-up ethos infiltrated me by some kind of familial osmosis. I was very aware of how hard he worked and of his commitment to do everything to the best of his ability. He faced lots of set backs, but never gave up until he achieved the success he always dreamed of. In this, my first race for a team, I had a very plausible and reasonable opportunity to settle for third, but my Dad wouldn't have settled for third without trying harder first. I am also sure that my mother would not have so done either. She was an only child from a rather Victorian family, which gave her a strong sense of right and wrong, independence, and a never-say-die attitude.

My lessons in the sport of running were coming thick and fast. Winning any kind of race feels good, but winning a race, which I thought I was going to lose, was considerably better. I now understood that the tougher the challenge, the infinitely more rewarding achievement became.

I certainly didn't win every time, because some of the schools we raced had better runners than me, but I always tried to win. I was playing rugby in the Christmas term, running cross-country and athletics in the Easter term, and playing cricket in the summer term. In my spare time I still played as much football as I could. On top of this, I started to go for runs as well. I liked the simple concept of effort and reward; if I did some training I would get better, and if I did more training I would get better still. It didn't amount to any sort of formal training, and I would often play football first and then run two or three miles afterwards.

This extra effort had the desired effect, and in my second year at Durham School, when I was 14 years old, I had improved enough to be picked for the senior school team. Suddenly, I was running against 17 year olds, and all prospects of winning my races came to an abrupt halt. Opinions in the school were divided about the concept of having a junior on the senior team, but not as divided as they were for one member of that senior team. My brother, Michael, was a regular member of the team. I suspect he was probably proud of his little brother when his little brother was winning junior races for the school, but it must have been galling for him to run for the school and have his little brother finish in front of him, especially as I sometimes prevented him from being a 'counter'.

A team consisted of eight runners and the fi rst six to fi nish on each team were counted for the team race. Your position in the race was your score; so fi rst place scored one point, second scored two, third scored three and so on. The team with the lowest score for their first six runners, or counters, was the winning team. If the points were tied, the position of the sixth runner, or last counter, was the deciding factor, because if our last counter beat their last counter, then our team had finished before their team and we won. Th is basic scoring system turned what is fundamentally an individual sport into an interesting and sometimes exciting team event. Th ere was obviously great competition at the front of the race among the potential winners, but the scoring system also created intense competition at the other end, because everybody wanted to be one of the counters.

National teams at the World Cross Country Championships use this same scoring system, except they have nine runners in a team. Competition to be a counter is intense there too because only the scoring six receive medals. If you are the seventh finisher for the World Championship winning team you leave with nothing, which is in stark contrast to the recent developments in football, where all the substitutes get a medal, the manager gets a medal, and before long the groundsman, bus driver, and tea lady will get a medal.

I was finishing third or fourth for the team, and Michael was usually sixth or seventh. Despite being beaten by his younger brother, Michael was just as keen on running as I was, and around this time he joined a running club. Ferryhill is in the middle of County Durham, and there were clubs on Tyneside, Wearside and Teeside, which were all equidistant from home. None of them was very convenient, but being a practical person, Michael joined Darlington Harriers for the simple reason that he was going out with a girl from Darlington. I wasn't going out with a girl from anywhere, so I joined Darlington Harriers too.

A new physical education teacher at school helped to bring a fresh perspective to my running. Nick Willings arrived, newly qualified, from Loughborough College. He was very enthusiastic and entered me in the London Athletic Club School's Championship. I was still a junior and the longest event for my age group was 400 metres. I thought going all the way to London to run 400 metres was pointless, but Mr Willings thought the experience of travelling there, and competing in a big meeting would be excellent experience for the future.

We duly travelled to London, and experienced the four hour train ride, the seedy bed and breakfast, and the long, long wait for my heat to start. I experienced the checking-in process of a large event, and the need to concentrate on my performance while long jumps, high jumps, throws and other races were all happening. I experienced the tension of going to the start, and the fear that comes from seeing all your rivals' tracksuits covered in badges; those badges that display such confidence sapping slogans as 'Surrey County Champion'. I experienced the burning, acid like fatigue that comes from running 400 metres flat out, and, as expected, I experienced a good drubbing as I finished comfortably last in my heat.

On the journey home, while we experienced a two hour delay for engineering works at Newark, Mr Willings simply assured me that next year I would be a senior and could run my real event, the 1,500 metres, where this year's experience would help me do well. When we travelled down the following year, we stopped at Loughborough to break the journey, and I met John Caine, who was in his last year as a student. He was a member of Gateshead Harriers, and he persuaded me to move from Darlington, and join Gateshead, where Stan Long was coaching a good group of young runners. John went on to run for England at Cross Country, and on the track in the Commonwealth Games. I went on from there to London and the LAC Schools 1,500 metres, which were held at Crystal Palace.

Crystal Palace was the home of British Athletics at the time, and it was exciting to run there, especially as it had a synthetic, all-weather track. I had only run on grass or cinder tracks before. Although I was nervous, I was at least familiar with waiting for my race, checking-in, warming-up and going to the start without being too distracted by all the activity around me. Unfortunately, I was also familiar with being soundly beaten, and I finished eighth in my heat in a time of 4 minutes 13 seconds.

This was 1969, and I had become sufficiently serious about my running to start a training diary on January 1st. I didn't actually do any training on January 1st, but I did record the fact that my idleness was due to the night before. I was running most days, but there was no structure or plan to my training. I liked to run fast, so I did lots of fast three-mile runs, and short hill repetitions. I had no goals beyond the next race, and no definite aspirations. I just had the simplistic concept of 'keep trying – get better.'

Mr Willings, however, did have aspirations for me, and the following year entered me again in the LAC Schools' Championship 1,500 metres at Crystal Palace. I was running well now, and I won my heat in a new personal best time of 4 minutes 4 seconds. Mr Willings told me I could win the final if I ran like that again. I wasn't sure, but I was sure I was going to try. The pace in the final felt quick from the start, but I stayed close to the front. The sound of the bell for the last lap startled me and I surged as hard as I could. I stole a few yards on everyone, and held on to the gap all the way round the last lap. I won in another personal best of 4 minutes 0.7 seconds, which equates to 4:19 for a mile. This was a major breakthrough. I went home with an enormous silver cup and even bigger grin on my face.

Two months later, I was running in Solihull at the English Schools' Championship. This is an enormous event, with a full programme of athletics for three different age groups. Everyone qualifies through his or her county championships, and each county is allowed two athletes per event. A particular county association will host it each year, and it therefore moves around the country. I was the second string for the combined team of Northumberland and Durham. We had a combined team because Northumberland is so sparsely populated. David Lowes was the first string, having beaten me by almost three seconds in the Durham County Championship.

The senior boys' 1,500m had two heats, with the winner from each heat and the six fastest losers going through to the final. I was thrilled when I won heat two, but soon realised I had been in much the weaker race as five of the six fastest losers came from heat one. Next day, when I stood on the start line, I was aware that I had only beaten one of these runners previously, and true to form I came second last. I ran within a second of my time at the LAC race, but this was a much higher level of competition. Lowes had finished third, and the winner was Ray Smedley, who went on to run internationally at every distance from 1,500m to the marathon.

I was eighteen, and this was the summer of my A levels. I was taking Chemistry, Physics and Biology. I wasn't particularly good at science subjects, but I had decided to be a pharmacist, and I had to take them. Obviously my father was a big influence on this decision. I found the whole subject of how medicines worked on the body very interesting, but I also wanted a professional job where I could have my own business. In the same way I preferred individual sports to team sports, I imagined I would like to be my own boss. My dad's business looked good to me, but I had little context in which to put it, as careers advice in those days was almost non-existent. I have no recollection of discussing alternative careers with anyone.

The career I would eventually take was something I didn't need to worry about for a little longer. Despite believing strongly in the ethos 'try hard –get better' when it came to my running, I failed to apply this to my studies and made a pig's ear of my exams. Without the required grades to get onto a Pharmacy degree course, I had to go to the local technical college and retake my A levels. This time I worked harder and got the results I needed.

A year of retakes may seem like a waste of time, but dark clouds have silver linings, and because I was still an A level student I was eligible for the English Schools' Championship. I was determined to improve on my previous second last, and was pleased to learn that this year's event was at Crystal Palace.

With hundreds of athletes coming from all over the country, the English Schools is a major logistical exercise. County Athletic Associations don't have the resources to put their teams in hotels, so local families are invited, or coerced, to look after two or three visiting athletes. I was billeted with two of my teammates to a semi-detached house in Penge. The lady of the house made us welcome and we were well fed. I cannot remember her name, but I do remember her clocks. She collected them, and had obviously done so for a long time. She had dozens and dozens of them. Some were big, and some were small, but all of them ticked, loudly. Not only did they tick, but they chimed too. Unfortunately, they didn't all keep good time, and the chiming of an hour, every hour, started at about five to and went on until nearly ten past. I couldn't contemplate getting to sleep until the cacophony of midnight had passed.

There were to be ten runners in the final this year, with the first two from each heat and the six fastest losers. I finished second in my heat to David Glassborrow from Warwickshire in 3 minutes 58 seconds. I felt reasonably comfortable throughout the race, and, if I could get some sleep, thought I would run really well in the final.

The next day was hot and sunny, and I had to sit for several hours in the stands waiting for my event. Whether it was the clock lady's food or just extreme nervousness, I don't know, but I was suffering from severe diarrhoea. It was probably nerves, because the problem disappeared when it came time to warm up. In contrast to a year earlier, I stood on the start line thinking I could beat all of these opponents if I ran well enough.

I was close to the front throughout the first two laps, which we ran in 2 minutes 5 seconds. It seemed quick enough to me, but Glassborrow went ahead and pushed on. I followed him. I was running hard and we reached the bell with a small gap behind us. He ran faster and faster, trying to break away from me down the back straight. My eyes were glued to his back as we hurtled round the last bend. There was a wall of noise coming from the stand as we hit the home straight. I moved slightly wide and started to sprint flat out. Within five yards I was on his shoulder, and I could see empty track ahead of me and the finish line eighty yards away. I thought, 'I'm going to win.'

It was so exciting to think I was going to win that something happened to me. My whole body tightened and I could no longer accelerate. I was on his shoulder, but I couldn't get past. For the last eighty yards we stayed the same, and I crossed the line still on his shoulder. We both smashed our personal bests. He ran 3:48.7 and I was second in 3:48.8. For the first, but not the last time in my career, I had to deal with the strange mixed emotions that came from running better than I thought I could, but still losing a race I wanted to win.

My consolation, and a big consolation at that, was being named with Glassborrow for the England team to compete against Scotland, Wales and Northern Ireland in the annual British Schools' International match. It was a week later at Meadowbank Stadium in Edinburgh, and my parents came to watch.

Glassborrow and I were the fastest runners in the race and we agreed to share the pace if nobody else would do the work. The first lap was a mediocre 65 seconds, so David took the second lap and I took the third. We ran 2:03 for those laps and had everybody else under pressure. He attacked on the back straight of the last lap and committed himself to the long sustained finish which had beaten me at Crystal Palace. He had a two-yard lead round the last bend, but coming into the straight I sprinted hard, and like the previous week, I was quickly on his shoulder. But I had learnt a valuable lesson. I concentrated on my running and kept the prospect and emotion of winning at bay. I went straight past him and won in 3:51.3 to his 3:52.0.

This was in the days before camcorders or digital cameras, but my dad had a video 8 movie camera, and he filmed the entire race for posterity. He carefully recorded each lap as the race unfolded, and had it perfectly focused as we hit the home straight. The crucial moment of the entire race was when I closed on Glassborrow and, by controlling my excitement, was able to go straight past.

My dad, as he watched it through the camera lens, wasn't able to control his emotions and the film goes suddenly from me catching Glassborrow to arcing views of the underside of the stadium roof as he flung his arms in the air in excitement.

CHAPTER 4

GATESHEAD

The Schools' International was my fi rst race at Meadowbank, but it wasn't my first visit to the Stadium. I had sat in the stands for a week, with my parents, a year earlier, as we watched the 1970 Commonwealth Games. My parents had never shown any particular interest in athletics before I started running, and I really appreciated them going there for my benefit.

We watched a lot of great athletes, but I especially wanted to see my hero of the time, Ron Clarke of Australia. He was a phenomenal runner, who had re-written the record books over 3 miles and 6 miles, without the aid of pacemakers. He won his races from the front by pushing harder and harder until no one could stay with him. In one race, he took half a minute off the world record for 10,000 metres. Unfortunately, he did not have a good sprint finish, and in the Tokyo Olympic Games of 1964, he couldn't drop Billy Mills or Mohammed Gamoudi, and they both sprinted past him in the finishing straight.

Four years later, when he was in the greatest form of his life, the Olympics were held at the 7,000 feet altitude of Mexico City. High altitude athletes dominated all of the distance events and the rarefied air robbed Clarke of any chance to run his best. He was carried away from the 10,000 metres on a stretcher, with an oxygen mask over his face.

He was about to retire, and these Commonwealth Games were his last chance to win a major title. I was enthralled as he led for lap after lap, and one by one the group got smaller. With three laps remaining, Dick Taylor of England and Lachie Stewart of Scotland were his only challengers. Clarke pushed on and Taylor was dropped. Every man, woman and child in the stadium was on the edge of their seats as Stewart hung on to the great Australian as they entered the last lap. Stewart was running the race of his life in front of his home crowd, and they all leapt from their seats as the Scot sprinted past in the last eighty yards.

The noise was deafening as they cheered home this unexpected Scottish victory. I sat still with a churning sensation in my stomach, because I had suddenly realised how harsh, and almost brutal, competitive sport could be. Clarke had been a much better runner than Stewart throughout his career, but now Stewart had a gold medal and Clarke still didn't. I looked at Clarke and thought 'you don't always get what you deserve.' But then I looked at Stewart and thought 'perhaps you can win anything if you are sufficiently inspired.'

Thanks to my meeting with John Caine in Loughborough, I was now a member of Gateshead Harriers, and the sight of John finishing fifth behind Lachie Stewart jolted me from my thoughts about Clarke. It felt good to be in the same running club as someone who ran in such amazing races. Later in the week, another Gateshead Harrier won the first of his large collection of major championship medals, when Brendan Foster took bronze in the 1,500 metres.

Gateshead Harriers had been formed in 1928. It had never won any major Club Championships, but it had a healthy membership, which now included a couple of international runners, and a large section of teenage runners. Stan Long coached the teenagers, and he was full of enthusiasm and optimism. He persuaded me to come through to Gateshead each Tuesday for the weekly Club training night.

By this time we had moved a couple of miles up the road from Ferryhill to Croxdale and before I had a car, I used to catch the bus to Gateshead, which was fifty minutes away. Our Tuesday night training venue in the winter was Coatsworth Road Junior School. The school didn't have changing rooms, so we used a classroom. Everything in a junior school is junior sized, and sitting on a toilet meant resting your chin on your knees. With no changing rooms, there were obviously no showers either, and after an hour of hard running round the dark, damp streets of Gateshead, you just can't beat getting washed with cold water in a pint sized basin, which is fixed to the wall just above knee level.

For a couple of months after I started going to Gateshead on Tuesday nights, I would wake up on Wednesdays with very stiff legs. I assumed it was because I was training harder than I was used to, but I now wonder if having a hot shower might have made a difference, instead of sitting on a bus for nearly an hour after washing myself in cold water.

Our summer training venue was Gateshead Stadium, but it was a different place then to the stadium that now hosts televised international athletics. A cinder track was surrounded by a steeply banked cycle racing track, and the grandstand seated all of fifty people. Nobody seemed too bothered about the facilities because the council had provided hundreds of miles of tarmac for us to run on, and in the winter they even made it floodlit.

I was sixteen when I joined Gateshead Harriers, and if I wasn't running for the school, I was running for the club in the Youths' age group. There were a few boys who could beat me at first, but I quickly developed, and soon there was only one who would regularly beat me in local road races. In a typical race, I would go the front and push the pace. I would eventually drop everybody except him, but with a hundred yards to go Mike McLeod would whoosh past me, get a gap, look around, and then hold me off till the finish. I found it very frustrating. If I had known that his exceptional sprint finish would eventually win him an Olympic 10,000 metre medal, I may have felt better about it. But at the time, I didn't.

I was collecting lots of little prizes during this stage of my career. I was getting a prize for finishing in the first three, and I was also getting a lot of team prizes as Gateshead usually won the team race. Entry fees for a Youths' road race were about 10p back then, so you couldn't really expect too much, but when you've got one tartan duffle bag you really don't need another one.

David Lowes, who I was to race often on the track, was a Gateshead teammate, and along with Ray Sterling and Derek Alderson, we had a good Youth team. Good enough, in fact, for Stan Long to think we had a chance of team medals in the National Cross Country Championship. I had no idea what the "National" was like, but everyone told me it was like nothing else I would ever run in.

In 1970 it was held at Blackpool Showground. All the best runners in the country were there, and they all wanted to get to the front when the race began. I had been warned to start fast, but I couldn't believe how everybody sprinted when the gun was fired. The start is extremely wide, but the course has to narrow and turn after 400 yards. If you are at the back when the course narrows, you will never be able to work your way through.

I had never been in a race with so many other runners. I spent the entire four miles in an ocean of arms and legs. I was continually passing people and being passed. Running hard in a dense crowd was so strange. I couldn't see more than a yard or two in front of me for bodies, and kept stumbling in dips and on tufts. I finished a very tired 28th, and second counter for Gateshead. All the team ran well and we finished second to Small Heath Harriers. Our silver medals were the first medals Gateshead had ever won in a national championship.

After my event I watched the senior race. There were no mass-running events at this time. A road race did well to attract 150 runners, but in the National Cross Country there were ten times as many. Almost every running club in the country sent a team, and every club had a place on the starting line. The start was divided into numbered pens, which were one runner wide. With a maximum of nine runners to a team, the best runner in each club would stand at the front, and his teammates had to line up behind him in their respective pens.

A big road race nowadays might be ten feet wide, and two or three hundred yards deep at the start, but the 'National' is ten feet deep and two or three hundred yards wide at the start. I stood a couple of hundred yards away from the line, and watched in amazement as a wall of runners hurtled towards me, all trying to make the first bend in a good position. The ground shook beneath my feet as they passed. Along with scores of other people, I ran from vantage point to vantage point to watch the leaders go by. I couldn't believe how fast these men ran, for nine miles, over rough ground.

Cross Country running could never be described as a glamorous sport, but on that day I was indelibly impressed by how everybody involved in it was so enthusiastic. They all talked in reverential terms about the leaders, but unfailingly encouraged every runner who went past. When they didn't know their names, they would recognise the colours of their vests and call them by their running clubs. Joining Gateshead

Harriers had expanded my sporting horizons so much and so quickly. On the coach journey home I felt infected with the same enthusiasm, although I suspect the little silver medal in my pocket had something to do with it.

Over the next two years I was running for the school with plenty of success, but I was now in the Junior age group for the club. Juniors ran in the Senior men's road races over six miles and I was well beaten in my first few events. Our Gateshead Harriers team was never able to repeat the success of Blackpool at the Junior National Cross Country, and I finished 37th at Norwich in 1971, and 23rd at Sutton Park the following year.

Saturday, March 4th 1972 at Sutton Park is a day never to be forgotten by anyone who was there. The Youths' race was run in quite reasonable conditions, but as we started in the Junior race, a cold front came blowing through; the temperature dropped to 33 degrees Fahrenheit; it rained hard and the wind blew. The term 'wind chill factor' was never heard then, but it was creating conditions equivalent to well below freezing, and we were running around soaking wet in our vests and shorts. On the part of the course directly into the wind, I had to run with my head down, looking just ahead of me. I knew that my friend, Dennis Coates of Middlesbrough, was about 20 yards in front of me, and I wanted to catch him. With my head down I pushed hard for a hundred yards; I looked up and Dennis was nowhere to be seen. I put my head down and battled on through a stream, which was swelling by the minute. I looked up again and he was there, 15 yards ahead. He had fallen head long into the stream, and been almost submerged when I had glanced up.

The ground was becoming soaked as the rain lashed down, and I fell twice during the last mile. The cold gripped me like a vice at the finish, and my hands were shaking too much to be able to take my racing spikes off my feet. The freezing rain came down throughout the entire nine miles of the Senior race.

The stream, which ran through the middle of the course, had been an easy jump for the youths, but took three or four strides to cross by the last lap of the men's race. At the finish line, I had never seen so many people shaking uncontrollably.

The changing rooms were at the nearest school, but it was over a mile away. People were so cold and so tired they couldn't walk back. Every passing car was stopped by runners, standing in the road, demanding to be taken to the school. It was the most extraordinary mass hijacking I have ever witnessed. Of course, the one thing everyone longs for, after such an experience, is a hot bath or shower. The school corridors were full of exhausted, semi-naked men looking for the shower room. It soon became apparent that there were no showers, but there were some baths. They were portable tin baths placed outside in a quadrangle, and filled by a fire hose. There were over a thousand dirty runners changing in the school, but nobody used those baths.

I had passed my A levels with appropriate grades by now, and I was in my first year of a Pharmacy degree course at Sunderland Polytechnic. There were about 60 of us in that year group, and being an active sportsman put me clearly in a minority of one. Much to the amusement of some of my fellow students, and a lot of the locals, I was running through the streets and parks of Sunderland every day. It was unusual in those days to see anyone running through the streets, and I would often have cars tooting their horns at me, or pedestrians shouting little gems of wit and repartee along the lines of 'Get your knees up!' or 'Have you missed the bus?' Depending on my mood I would either ignore them, or simply indicate that I had two miles left to run.

I ran on the track for Gateshead Harriers that summer and ran around 4 minutes 6 seconds for the mile on a few occasions. I was running well enough, but I was competing with the men now, and it was very hard to win anything. During my last year at school I had run 42 races and won 19 of them. In the next two years I ran 62 races, but won only nine times. Runners who have enjoyed success at school often find the transition to senior level difficult, especially with the additional distractions of student life. I certainly preferred winning to losing, but because I was only a short drive away from Gateshead, I was able to thrive on the enthusiasm and attitudes of every one at the club each Tuesday night. I was frequently told how it takes time to become a good senior runner, and I was happy to accept it.

General enthusiasm wasn't the only influence on me. I was regularly training with John Caine, a track and cross-country international; Bill Robinson, a cross country international; and Brendan Foster, who by now had bronze medals from both the Commonwealth Games and European Championships at 1,500 metres. Young runners often regard international athletes as creatures from a superior species, who possess powers and talents that are denied to ordinary mortals. I may have thought the same way if I hadn't mingled with them on a weekly basis, but because I ran with them so regularly, I rather naively adopted a different attitude. My club-mates were going away to run in major championships, so I assumed that this was the natural thing to do. Thanks to their achievements, I quietly, almost sub-consciously, adopted very high expectations for myself. These expectations took a very long time to fulfil, but they were definitely formed in my early days at Gateshead Harriers, thanks to the presence of people like Brendan Foster.

Although that environment helped me a lot, I often found it daunting to train with Brendan. Apart from being a better runner than me, he also had far more self confidence than I did. Over the next few years I learnt some of his techniques. When I was about to run some big race and felt concerned about how many good runners I was up against, he would say that I could dismiss half of them, because half of them would beat themselves with nerves; that would only leave half and surely I could beat half of them. Once, when he wasn't very fit but was about to run a big event, we asked what he was going to do. He replied that he would have to 'borrow one.' When asked to explain, he said it was like going to the bank for a loan; he would have to win the race and then do the training afterwards.

Brendan made the team for his third major championship in three years, when he was selected for the Munich Olympics. I usually watch the Olympic Games on television, (because, as Eddie Izzard said, they have never held them outside my bedroom window), but in 1972 I drove to Germany with Steve Walker to watch the ultimate athletics event. Steve was a long-haired, scruffy, beer drinking, music loving runner from Middlesborough, so, apart from our football allegiances, we had a great deal in common. Unfortunately, one thing we didn't have in common was a driving license, so I had to drive the 1,500 miles there and the 1,500 miles back again. There were no hotel rooms to be had in Munich, and the nearest accommodation we could find was in a little Bavarian village 45 minutes drive from the stadium. My car was a brown and beige Riley Kestrel, and it struggled with the intense heat on the German autobahns. On the warmest days, we had to drive with the heater on full blast to take heat away from the engine, to prevent it from boiling over.

We had tickets for every session of the athletics, and we sat through every round of every event. We really lapped it up, if that's not too bad a pun to use. I had presumed that people sitting in the Olympic Stadium would all be track and field fans, but I was quickly proved wrong. Just before the first heat of the first event, an American sitting in front of us turned to me and asked, 'Hey Bud, which way round do they go?'

I particularly remember seeing Brendan Foster finish 5th in the 1,500 metres when Kip Keino of Kenya was surprisingly beaten by Vasala of Finland; and how Keino won the 3,000 metre steeplechase when he wasn't expected to. I remember David Bedford trying to win the 10,000 metres with aggressive front running, and how Finland's Lasse Viren won that race, even though he was tripped and fell at half way. I was impressed by how smooth Frank Shorter looked when he ran into the stadium to win the marathon, and even more impressed by Viren, who completed an incredible double when he won the 5,000 metres.

Mary Peters won Britain's only athletics gold medal in the pentathlon, but Foster was 5th in the 1,500 metres, and Ian Stewart, who I had watched win the Commonwealth Games, was 3rd in the 5,000 metres. Bedford was 6th in 10,000 metres and Ron Hill was also 6th in the marathon. We didn't have any distance running world-beaters, but we did have world-class runners at all the distance events. As I watched all this drama unfold, I privately wondered if I would ever emulate any of these heroes.

During the long drive home, I committed myself to moving my running career forward. I was determined to train more consistently, and to achieve higher levels of performance. As my second year at Sunderland polytechnic began, I was into my winter training, and feeling very committed. There was no college running club, but the student's union was very helpful to any individuals who wanted to compete in external polytechnic events. I entered the British Polytechnic Cross Country Championships as Sunderland's only representative, and trained hard for it, believing that I had an excellent chance of winning. A British Championship of any sort was exactly the step forward I wanted to make.

The race was in Liverpool on the third Sunday of January, and to make sure I was fully rested and could run my best, I drove there the day before. I booked into a hotel and looked forward to a good night's sleep. Unfortunately, the heating wasn't working, and it was an incredibly cold night. There were no spare blankets in my room and I just couldn't get to sleep. I eventually warmed up after taking the curtains down from the window and using them as blankets. Undeterred by a restless night, I had a good breakfast and wandered around Liverpool to while away the morning. Giving myself plenty of time, I set off for the course with determination and high hopes. I had a map of the location, sent by the organisers, who, from the pre-race information, seemed to have everything under control. I was a little surprised that the streets were so quiet as I approached, and even more surprised to see nobody at all on the course, except a farmer in his tractor ploughing the land precisely where my map said 'Start'.

I checked my information again. I checked the date, and I checked the name of the road. This was definitely the right day, time and place, but there again, quite definitely it wasn't. After scratching my head for a while, I had no alternative but to get back in my car and drive the three and half hours home, having been to Liverpool for the joy of shivering all night under a pile of curtains. I bumped into the secretary of the Student Union the following day.

'Did you get my message?' he asked.

'What message was that?' I said.

'The one about them changing the race to Saturday.'

All my training, however, was not in vain. I was driving to Gateshead every Tuesday night to run a gruelling ten miler with the club's best runners. All through the winter of 1972-73 we discussed the same thing on those Tuesday runs, and we all made a commitment to aim for the National Cross Country team title. The club had never won a national title, but we believed we had a team that might just do it, and every week, as we hammered round the dark streets, we talked about how we were good enough.

Bill Robinson, John Caine and Brendan Foster were all established internationals. Lindsay Dunn was a 4:06 miler and winner of plenty of local road races. John Trainor was a former Northern Counties Boys' Champion and Peter Parker was the club captain. I was now old enough to run in the senior race, and hoped I could handle nine miles of country at my first attempt.

The race was in London, at Parliament Hill Fields on the edge of Hampstead Heath. We had to run three laps of three miles each. I had seen the start of a senior 'National' for the first time three years earlier at Blackpool, and I had been impressed with it. I now realised that it was considerably more impressive, or frightening, when I was in the middle of it. The first four hundred yards were uphill, but that didn't deter anyone from setting off as if it was a mile race. I knew I had to start fast, and got carried along by the surge and momentum of people around me.

We had all worked hard for this race, and I wasn't going to let anyone down. I wanted to be part of a winning team, so I raced round the first lap as fast as I could. There were always plenty of spectators counting the runners, and shouting out the places, as we went past. I was 33rd going into the second lap, and Stan Long was urging me on because we were just leading the team race.

My efforts on the first circuit were now taking their toll. I was breathing hard, and my legs were aching. It was a hilly course, and on every climb a couple of runners would come past me. I was struggling, but I had to keep plugging away. I knew I was losing places but I seemed unable to do anything about it. At the end of the second lap I had slipped to 47th, and Stan was urging me on because the team was in second place.

With one lap to go I made up my mind that nobody

else was going to pass me, but ten yards later a runner came up beside me. It was John Caine, who had started more slowly, but was now working his way through. He urged me to work together with him. I stuck to him and we passed one and then another. Suddenly, I was feeling better; I was still tired and working hard, but we were moving through, and nobody was passing us. It was easier to push myself on with John as my pacemaker.

The race was won by New Zealander Rod Dixon, who had won a bronze medal at Munich the year before. More importantly for us, Bill Robinson finished 6th and Brendan Foster was 12th to give the team a terrific start. With half a mile to go, John pressed on harder than I could manage and he finished 34th as I hung on for 36th. Four of our six counters had now finished, but more than sixty runners crossed the line behind me without the sight of a red and white Gateshead vest. Bolton Harriers were our biggest rivals and by now they had six runners home.

With about a mile to go, Peter Parker was our next runner, followed closely by John Trainor. Lindsay Dunn was out of any medals we might win because he was seventh counter. They were all pushing hard for the finish, and they all knew there were two possible medals for the three of them. John passed Peter. Lindsay knew he would miss out unless he could move up. They were all passing other runners, but it was beating each other that motivated them. Lindsay took Peter with half a mile to go. John finished 107th, and with Lindsay in 109th place, we had a team total of 304 points. It took ages to confirm Bolton's score, but their positions added up to 310, and we had won the National Cross Country Team Title by six points.

The trophy is a very old, very large, and very beautiful silver cup. It may not be as famous as the FA Cup, but the champagne we drank out of it on the train from Kings Cross to

Newcastle could not have tasted better. We had dreamt about winning this title for a long time; we had worked together through a lot of dark, cold winter nights; and even though running is such an individual sport, we had truly become a team for this event. We had shared the commitment, and the training, and it was a wonderful feeling to share the victory, and the pints of champagne, with everybody from the club on that journey home. In fact, we shared it with everybody in that railway carriage whether they were from Gateshead Harriers or not.

CHAPTER 5

I NEARLY DIED

When I was 23 years old I almost died. There was a moment when my life could have ended in about the time it takes for Usain Bolt to run 200 metres, if I hadn't received the right medication. But, as I will explain a little later, I got the correct treatment in the nick of time. When I recovered from this incident, I adopted an attitude of 'I nearly died, but I didn't, so that's ok', but the experience left me with an enhanced appreciation of life. I think we all tend to take life for granted until we are faced with death. It also increased my appreciation of running, because running always makes me feel so alive.

Running is one of the best sports to be involved in when things are going well. I know it requires a lot of discipline and commitment, but that is part of its appeal to those who enjoy it. Things that come too easily are seldom highly valued, but it can be immensely satisfying when you commit yourself to something, work diligently towards it, and then have to perform well to achieve it.

Running well depends on two things. Physical fitness is the first and most obvious criteria; your talent, or natural ability, will determine your level of competition. Within that level, anyone can excel by training well enough to reach peak fitness.

Ability to perform is the second criteria to running well. It depends on confidence, determination and motivation. When the Tuesday night group at Gateshead Harriers decided to try to win the National Cross Country title, we committed ourselves to it. We trained hard for it, and, more importantly, everyone performed to his utmost on the day, because we believed we could do it, and we wanted to do it. The victory didn't come easily, but that is why it was so satisfying and rewarding. The same sense of achievement can be enjoyed at any level of running, as long as you have strived to succeed.

Some of the training can be arduous, but the pure action of running becomes a joy when you are fit and well. There are few better feelings in life than running smoothly along a soft forest path, on a bright spring day, with the dappled sunshine glinting on a babbling brook, and the fresh, blossom-scented air filling your lungs. When the ground just flows beneath your feet for mile after mile, you feel tireless, fit, strong, and wonderfully alive. Running is a terrific sport when things are going well: but when things are going badly, it can be really dire.

If you are injured and can't compete it is just as frustrating for a runner as for a footballer, cricketer or golfer, but when you come back from injury in those other sports, you can usually play straight away. You may not be at your very best, but you can have an enjoyable and satisfying game or round. You can always make a good pass, hit a four, or sink a long putt without being on top form. Running a race depends so much on physical fitness, and if you are an unfit runner, who records slow times and loses to people who have never beaten you before, it is hard to find a section of the race you are satisfied with. When you are unfit that forest footpath is all uphill, the sunshine is too warm, the stream is too noisy, and the blossom makes you sneeze.

My first experiences of running taught me that if I

trained I became fitter, and if I trained more, I became fitter still. Injuries are bound to happen to every sportsman at some time, so they shouldn't be a real problem if they are handled correctly. The first step is to try to avoid them, but when they occur they should be treated. When they are over, some good training will make them seem like an irrelevant interruption. You don't need to stay unfit for long when injuries have set you back, as long as you can start training again.

The problem occurs when you suffer an injury, recover, fight your way back to fitness, and then get injured again. If this process becomes a regular cycle, you can never build on your fitness level. To improve significantly you need to achieve a certain level, maintain it until it becomes your natural level, and then move on to a higher level. If you keep suffering injuries, progress is always interrupted.

I was 19 when I first developed a sore Achilles tendon in February 1972. After some treatment and a week's rest, I was fine until April, when I had to take three days off to let some soreness settle down. I was living in a student bed-sit in Sunderland, training once every day, and covering about 55 miles per week. I was injury free until May the following year, when I had another flare up of my left Achilles tendon, which cleared after a week's rest. These were short-term, minor injuries and had no effect on my progress.

In the summer of 1973, I improved my best mile time to 4 minutes 4.0 seconds on a five-laps-to-the-mile cinder track at South Shields. I reduced my 1,500 metres time to 3:45.3 in the heats of the AAA Championships, and ran 8:35 for two miles at Crystal Palace. Brendan Foster won the latter race with a new world record of 8:13.8. I was in second place with 200 yards to go but was out-sprinted by Chris Stewart and Bernie Ford. I was thrilled with my time, and very excited to be in a world record setting race. I was 21 years old and felt excited about the future.

Lindsay Dunn had recently moved to Newcastle and I got to know him around this time because we trained together at Gateshead on Tuesday nights. He had lived with Brendan Foster when they had both been in Leeds, and was helping Brendan with his training programme. He was very excited about my 8:35 for two miles, and wanted to know what training I was doing. We often discussed training after that, and although Lindsay never formally coached me, this was the start of a relationship which was to guide my whole career.

1974 was the year of my final exams and I worked hard enough to gain my degree. To become a fully qualified pharmacist, I had to complete a year of work under the supervision of a suitably qualified pharmacist. My plan had been to work in, and then take over, my father's business, but before I did that I decided to do my post graduate year in a London Hospital, to gain a far wider range of experience. I shared a house in Golders Green with five other newcomers to London, and I got a job at St Thomas' Hospital, where, much to the delight of a lad from Ferryhill, I was able to time my tea-breaks on Big Ben, as the hospital is directly across the river from the Houses of Parliament.

My professional life was moving forward as it should, but my running career was not. I suffered another tendon flare up in the summer, which meant no track races at all, and resulted in a nine week period when I didn't run a step. Throughout the entire year, I averaged only 38 miles per week. The extended rest took all the inflammation from my tendon, and I was pain free when I started running again in the autumn. Lindsay Dunn was in touch to see how I was doing and insisted that, if I was pain free, I needed to step up to training twice a day all the time.

Throughout the winter of 1974 to 1975, I was running twice a day on Monday to Saturday, with one long run on

Sunday. St Th omas' is a teaching hospital and the medical students had a locker room with showers, which I was able to use by pretending to be a medical student. I would go to work on the underground, with my running kit and a change of underwear and shirt. After work, I would store my clothes in a locker, and run the eight miles home. I would run back to work the following morning, shower and change into my clean clothes. I did this twice a week with all my other runs done from home. It took me 50 minutes to run from home to work, but it usually took 55 minutes to get from door to door when I went on the Northern Line. I was, therefore, saving both time and money, despite the obvious drawback of trying to run across Westminster Bridge and Parliament Square in the rush hour.

I trained well all winter and drove up to Luton in March to meet my Gateshead colleagues for the National Cross Country Championships. I had been 46th in the National the previous year, but felt sure I could improve on that, and play my part in helping the team to regain the National title. Luton was the sort of course that suited me. It had one big hill each lap but the rest of it was flat, grassy and dry. The race was won by a Luton athlete, Tony Simmons, who went on to be fourth in the Montreal Olympic 10,000 metres the following year. I ran the best cross country race of my career and finished twelfth. I was first counter for Gateshead's winning team, and after the race I discovered that two of the men in front of me were Scottish. I hadn't even thought about the fact that this race was the trial for the World Cross Country Championships, and with nine men in the team, I was named travelling reserve because I was tenth Englishman. I had won myself a trip to Rabat in Morocco. I was so pleased with the day that I went back to Gateshead, on the bus, with the rest of the team to enjoy the celebration. I had to get the train back to London the next day, then another train to Luton, followed by a bus and finally a long walk to get my car back.

Travelling reserve to Morocco sounds like a nice holiday, and in many ways it was, but it was a strange position to be in. I had to assume I was running, even warm up before the race, in case anyone dropped out at the last moment. I was very pleased nobody did, because two days after Luton my Achilles tendon had started hurting again, and although I was able to run on it, I knew another hard cross country race was not going to help it. The race was won by Ian Stewart, who had won the European indoor 3,000m title a few weeks earlier.

I had several weeks of treatment and easy jogging, which settled it down, as it had done before. By May I was training and racing, but in the middle of June it became very sore again, and I stopped running completely for a week. The time had come for some drastic action, so I arranged to see Dr John Williams, an orthopaedic surgeon in Slough. He had operated successfully on John Caine's tendons, and it was John who recommended him to me.

The tendon was extremely tender when touched, and Dr Williams thought he should operate and decompress the tendon by removing the scar tissue around it. He couldn't do it until August, but suggested that I keep running. It might clear up by itself, but if I made it worse it didn't really matter.

My week of rest had helped, and I was able to run again without any significant trouble. I trained hard in the hope I could salvage something from the track season, knowing that I would soon have the problem solved. I finished second in a mile race in 4:06.5, and two weeks later came back to Gateshead for the Gateshead Games. Brendan Foster had broken the World record for 3,000m at this meeting 12 months earlier, and was attempting the 5,000 metre record this time. The stadium was packed and the atmosphere was fantastic.

I ran the 3,000 metres, and was amazed to reel off

laps in 63 seconds. I was second to Ian Stewart at the bell, and although I was out-sprinted in the last lap, I finished fourth in 7 minutes 54 seconds. This was a personal best by a long way and a considerable breakthrough in my level of performance. Several people told me I obviously didn't need an operation if I could run like that, and I began to wonder if a miracle might happen and I could avoid the surgeon's knife.

When I woke the next morning, I lay in bed for a while remembering how well I had run the day before, but when I got up my tendon was so sore I couldn't even walk properly, let alone run. I didn't run at all for the next four weeks, as I waited for surgery. I was admitted to Taplow Hospital on August 26th, with my operation scheduled for the next day.

I had an antiseptic bath, and a nurse shaved my lower leg. I put on one of those strange back-to-front operating gowns all hospitals use, and I was wheeled into the anteroom, where the anaesthetist prepared me for the operation. I was lying on my back as he explained that he would give me an injection of short-acting barbiturate, which would put me to sleep. He would then give me the full anaesthetic before I was taken into the operating theatre, but I would know nothing about it until I woke up back in the ward, lying on my stomach. He warned me that my leg would be hurting, but he would arrange some strong painkillers to take care of that.

He said he would count to three as he injected Thiopentone into a vein in my arm, but I only heard the one and the two. You cannot fight that injection like you can fight sleep; it just knocks you out. I felt very strange the next time I was aware of anything. I was slowly emerging from a deep sleep, and I was confused. Several different things confused me. I was lying on my back. I had intense pains in my head and groin. I was breathing into a mask held over my mouth. I tried to open my eyes, but I couldn't.

I was becoming more conscious now, and I was aware of a lot of people in the room, and a lot of agitated voices. As I tried again to open my eyes, the mask was removed from my mouth and a woman's voice, close to my ear, said, "Can you hear me?" I told her I could, and she continued, "Don't try to open your eyes. They are too swollen. How do you feel?"

As I was telling her where I was hurting, someone came rushing into the room, and demanded to know, "What have you given him?"

A different voice said, "Adrenaline, prednisolone, chlorpheniramine and oxygen. His blood pressure was 80 over 20, but it's 90 over 40 now."

I felt indescribably bad. My heart was pounding in my chest, and there was confusion all around me, but something registered in my brain. It was only a year since I had taken my pharmacy degree finals, and I recognised that list of drugs as standard treatment for anaphylactic shock. Suddenly I felt better, because I knew what was happening to me.

Later, I was to appreciate that I have an exceptional ability to look on the bright side. I was feeling better about what was happening now that I knew what it was. Someone less optimistic than me may have dwelled on the other things I knew about anaphylactic shock. It is a rare, allergic reaction, and is similar to the reaction caused by a bee sting. The big difference is that the swelling caused by a bee sting is localised, but in anaphylaxis the swelling is happening to the whole body. Liquid that should be in the blood stream leaks out into the gaps between the cells, causing huge swelling, especially around the eyes. When the blood volume goes down, the pressure goes down too, and the heart beats faster and faster to keep blood flowing. If you don't get treatment very quickly, anaphylactic shock will probably kill you.

The sedative effect of the thiopentone injection only

lasts a few minutes, and I had started to wake up in the middle of the allergic reaction. The fact that I woke up at all was reassuring and I assumed I was going to be fine. When my pulse and blood pressure stabilised, I was taken to the Cardiac Intensive Care unit, where I drifted in and out of sleep for an hour or two. When I became more awake, I began to realise the implications. My operation had obviously been cancelled, and I was glad to have discovered this allergy before a minor operation, rather than something more urgent and critical. Having an anaphylactic shock when your appendix has just burst would not be a good idea!

My systems had settled down, and I was feeling a little closer to normal, but there were still some concerns. I had to drink measured amounts of water every hour for the rest of the day, and throughout the night, to see if my kidneys were still working properly. They can easily be damaged by a lack of blood supply, and the doctors were worried this may have happened during my reaction. Thanks to the sophisticated medical process of measuring the volume of my urine, I was declared fit enough to be transferred to a cardiac ward, where I spent three days with a dozen old men who were recovering from heart attacks.

While I was there, the anaesthetist came to see how I was, and to tell me what had happened. After the thiopentone, he had injected me with Scoline, which is a muscle relaxant. It is needed to counteract the convulsions, which are triggered by one of the levels of unconsciousness you descend through when having a general anaesthetic. He had turned away to prepare the next injection, but when he looked at me again he thought my 'ear lobes looked a little blue'. He checked my pulse and blood pressure, but couldn't get a reading because the former was rising and the latter was falling too quickly. My face was starting to swell, and luckily for me, he knew exactly what was happening, and more importantly, knew what to do about it.

He felt that if he hadn't spotted the colour of my ears for another twenty seconds, it might have been too late. He told me that he had never lost a patient, but for about a minute he thought he was going to lose me. I found that all the medical staff preferred to talk about misplacing me, rather than say 'you nearly died'.

At a later date, I had to go the dermatology department of the Royal Victoria Infirmary in Newcastle to undergo allergy skin tests. I had been given two injections, and although everybody expected it to be the barbiturate I was allergic to, we had to make sure, so that I could avoid it in the future. A tiny amount of each drug was injected into the skin on my forearm. A large weal, just like a bee-sting, formed at the site of the Scoline injection. They were so surprised and excited by it, I was paraded, or rather my arm was paraded, around half a dozen departments of the hospital. They even called for a photographer, and I assume that my arm, with a large lump on it, now adorns the inside of some medical textbook.

I was told that being allergic to Scoline was a one in a million chance, and people say that winning an Olympic medal is also a one in a million chance. What I want to know is - how come I've never won the lottery?

I recovered fully from the reaction, and spent two weeks at home, before going back to Taplow Hospital to have my postponed Achilles tendon operation. Neither Dr Williams nor I wanted to risk a repeat of my previous experience, so he decompressed my tendon under local anaesthetic. I discovered that he operated while listening to classical music; the procedure took about 15 minutes; and it was very important to keep still. It was a strange sensation. I felt no pain, but I was aware of him touching my tendon and poking about inside my leg.

When he had finished, I was taken back to the ward feeling really good. I felt like the whole thing was no trouble at all, until the local anaesthetic wore off. Then it hurt more than I can describe, and I spent most of the night biting my pillow so as not to cry out in pain.

After four days in hospital, I was transferred to Farnham Park Rehabilitation Centre. Dr Williams would only operate on people who agreed to undergo a full rehabilitation programme afterwards. It was important to get mobility back in the tendon as quickly as possible, so that adhesions and scars from the surgery couldn't attach to the tendon. I was keen to be back on my feet, but I went into Farnham Park feeling very sorry for myself, because my leg was sore and I was hopping around on crutches.

It took me less than 24 hours to put my position into perspective. There were a few other sportsmen recovering from operations, but most of the people in Farnham Park were recovering from accidents. I shared a dining table with two men learning to walk again. One had lost a leg, and the other had his pelvis crushed when he fell between a moving train and the platform at Paddington station.

There was a 9 am to 4 pm timetable of daily activities and exercises, and the physio-terrorists, as we called them, were relentless in their pursuit of improvement. I was there for four weeks of gruelling work. I went in unable to put my foot on the ground, but I came out doing shuttle runs and circuit training.

It had been July 26th 1975 when I made my breakthrough at 3,000 metres in Gateshead, but it was October 14th before I was able to run another step. I went home on the 19th and began the very long and slow process of getting back to fitness and full training.

My post graduate year was over; I was a fully qualified and registered pharmacist, and I was working fulltime in my father's business in Ferryhill. I slowly increased my training and I worked my way up to running 70 miles per week by

December. In January 1976 I developed plantar fascitis, which causes pain in the arch of the foot, and by February I was doing 20 miles a week. It cleared up in March in time for me to turn out for Gateshead's defence of the National Cross Country title in Leicester. We won the team race again, but I finished in 95th place, and as I was 7th counter, it was the six team-mates in front of me who won the medals. This was quite a come down from leading the team home in 12th place a year earlier.

I improved during the spring and early summer, and in June I went to Switzerland with Lindsay Dunn for ten days of altitude training at Pontresina near St Moritz. Lindsay has his own, distinct ideas about altitude training, which I will discuss in detail later. We ran some brisk runs through beautiful forests and gasped for air in track sessions, and when we got back to London and went out for a 5 mile spin, we ended up laughing out loud because we were going so fast and feeling so easy.

Although we were only at high altitude for ten days, I am sure it worked because in the next few weeks I ran my best ever mile of 4 minutes 3.5 seconds, followed by my best 2 miles of 8 minutes 26 seconds. I also slashed my best for 5,000m with 13:40.7 when I finished third to Brendan Foster and Nick Rose in the AAA Championship. With that run, I won my first Great Britain vest, as opposed to an English Cross County vest, when I was selected to run in an international 5,000m road race in Belgrade.

It is always a major landmark for anybody to get their first Great Britain vest, and I was very excited when I arrived at the old Amateur Athletic Association office in Brompton Road. I was presented with a size medium, pristine vest and introduced to my team manager. I was the only athlete on this trip, but I still had to have a team manager, because every team had to have a team manager. It appeared that on low key internationals like this one, they shared the team manager jobs around a group of elderly, but stalwart servants of the sport. And if you had never been abroad before, you went to the top of the list.

A couple of hours before the race, I got all my racing kit out and carefully removed the treasured vest from its cellophane wrapping. I tried it on, but it seemed extremely tight, and I realised that I had been given a pristine, size medium, Great Britain women's running vest. I could have used this as an excuse for my disappointing 12th place finish, but the truth is, I just didn't run very well. We travelled home the next day. My team manager was a nice enough man, but I fear that he would still be trying to find his way around Belgrade airport if I hadn't been there to look after him.

During the following winter, Gateshead Harriers were aiming for their fourth National Cross Country team title in five years, but we were concerned that we would need our very best team because there was stiff opposition. Brendan Foster didn't want to run because it didn't really fit in with his plans. Somehow, it became my job to persuade him to run, and I did a variety of calculations and projections to predict our rivals possible scores, and what we would score with and without him. I assured him that he and I could have a combined score of 40 points, which should clinch it for us.

Quite remarkably, I predicted our combined score exactly, although I had never contemplated what actually happened. I believe Brendan is still grateful to me for persuading him to run, so that he could add National Cross Country Champion to his list of honours, and if you remember how team scoring works from Chapter 3, you will have already worked out that I finished 39th. I was disappointed with my run, but it was enough for another team title.

I felt that I wasn't making enough progress and I needed to take my training to a higher level. During June of 1977 I ran weekly track sessions which included 4 x 800m in an average time of 2:03.7; 8 x 400m in 59.7; and 3 x 1600m in 4:17. I did the latter session on a Saturday morning while my Dad worked at the Pharmacy, and I worked in the afternoon while he had time off. I can still remember the intense pain in my right Achilles tendon as I hobbled around the dispensary that day. The intense track sessions had been too much for my fragile lower leg, and over the next nine weeks, the most I managed was a 3 mile jog.

I went back to see Dr Williams and he put me on the waiting list for a repeat of the operation he had done on my left leg. In the meantime, I wore raised heels, took anti-inflammatory tablets, had ultra-sound treatment and regularly plunged my sore heel in and out of buckets of alternately hot and cold water. After a month of this routine, I was able to increase my running slowly and by October I was doing 70 miles per week without any pain. I phoned Dr Williams and postponed the operation as I seemed to be alright. In November I won the North Shields road race, and in December ran for England in a cross country race in Marseilles, where I led and dropped everybody except for a Tunisian, who, as usual, out-sprinted me at the finish. This was a good run and things were looking up.

During my year in London, I occasionally ran with Brendan Foster's brother, Peter. When I returned to the North East, he went to Kenya to work as a Voluntary Service Overseas (VSO) teacher. He was based at a Catholic school in Iten, which had produced a remarkable string of world-class runners. Iten is almost 7,000 feet above sea-level, and Peter invited me to visit him and do some high altitude training.

I really liked the idea, because I had run so well the summer after Lindsay and I had been to Switzerland and I wanted to have another really good track season. The trip was arranged for late March, 1978, and I went with Barry Smith as my training partner. We flew to Nairobi and tried to hire a car.

An ex-patriot Englishman ran the company we dealt with, but he wasn't happy when we told him where we were going. Iten is about 30 miles from Eldoret, and Eldoret is the only place for a hundred miles that could possibly be described as a town. It is a good four hours drive from Nairobi to Eldoret, and the roads get worse the further from the capital you go. This guy only hired his cars to people who wanted to drive around Nairobi.

We played the patriotism card as best we could. We told him, in passionate terms, that we were two British athletes trying to break into the British team; we were here to do four weeks of altitude training, and we had to have a car. He eventually wavered and allowed us to drive away in a six month old Ford Escort, after promising, with our hands on our hearts, that we would look after it. Luckily, neither he, nor I, had the faintest idea what sort of roads we would end up driving on.

There were no motorways or dual carriageways in Kenya in those days, and the main road north to Eldoret was hundreds of miles of regular two-lane road. From Eldoret we turned east towards Iten, which stands on the edge of the Rift Valley. Ten miles out of Eldoret the tarmac stopped, and from there the roads were made of distinctive, hard-packed, ochre-coloured soil.

St Patrick's School at Iten consisted of a series of single storey brick buildings with corrugated iron roofs. These were the first brick buildings we had seen since Eldoret. Peter's bungalow had a panoramic view of the undulating countryside, and as we sat on his front porch recovering from the journey, I gazed at miles of jumbled blotches of deep brown and green. At first it looked like a chaotic wilderness, but with time, and Peter's help, I was able to pick out at first a few, and then dozens, of mud huts spread throughout a patchwork of tiny fields. This was populated and cultivated land, but there were no chimneys, no walls, no pylons, no cables or wires across the sky, and everything was either green or brown.

The children who came to Peter's school all lived in mud huts, and their families farmed tiny pieces of land. Swahili was their native tongue, but they took lessons in English, and sat examinations set by English exam boards. Peter taught geography, and although most of them had never been more than ten miles from home, they accepted everything Peter told them about the world, except for one thing. Apparently, they just could not accept that places like Greenland and the South Pole were permanently covered in snow. They knew what snow was, but if it lay on the ground, surely it would melt.

In our attempts to emulate the great runners this school had produced, Barry and I took our first high altitude training run. For the first couple of miles we ran comfortably along the dirt road, wondering what all the fuss was about. Then we came to a hill. It wasn't a particularly long or steep hill, but the minor increase in effort to get up it had us gasping for breath. One of the best measures of physical fitness is how quickly you recover from being out of breath, but we ran down the other side and along the level still gasping for breath.

As the days went by, we either acclimatised or simply got used to running while gasping for breath, because it never seemed quite so bad again. We ran along the edge of the Rift Valley and through forests with monkeys swinging in the trees above our heads. This was definitely not a tourist area, and outside of the school, it was very rare for the local people to see a white face, not to mention our white legs and arms. One day we were several miles away from Iten, running along a small path, when we came up behind a barefoot man in rags carrying a large sack on his back. He heard us just before we caught him, turned to see who it was, then smiled and said, 'Good morning.' We returned his 'good morning' in what was a quite surreal encounter.

Peter shared his house with Shaun, a fellow teacher. They both thought St Patrick's was a good place to work because between 7 and 9 pm every evening they had electricity, supplied by the school generator. They also had a cook by the name of Sang, who made them a meal each night, and baked extremely good bread. After about a week of evenings spent talking or reading, we thought we deserved a little relaxation, so we left Sang to make dinner and Barry, Peter, Shaun and I drove two miles down the road to a little village that had a bar.

This village was just a row of seven or eight rectangular wooden huts lined up beside the road. It resembled something from a Western B movie, and all it lacked was a hitching rail and tumbleweed. One of these huts was the bar. It was a basic wooden room with a couple of wooden tables and chairs, and a wooden counter at the back of the room. It served the full range of Kenyan brewed beers, which was a choice between a bottle of Tusker and a bottle of White Cap. The only other drink they served was Chi. Chi was made by putting cold water, milk, tea and sugar in a pan, and boiling it. We all decided to have beer.

After our first beer, we did the sociable thing and had a second. After the second, we thought we ought to be getting back because Sang would have dinner ready. We hadn't told him exactly when we would be back, so the consensus of opinion was that we should have a quick third beer, and then go. We had almost finished our drinks, when two Kenyans walked into the bar. One was better dressed than the other, and he greeted Peter warmly. They talked for a while in Swahili, and when the Kenyans went to the bar, Peter explained that he had been talking to Josephat, who was one of the local chiefs.

Apparently, Josephat held St Patrick's school in high esteem, and because Barry and I were visitors to his village, he was going to buy us a drink. All four of us felt that we had already had just the right amount of beer, but Peter made it clear that this was an honour and it would be inexcusably rude to refuse. We had to have this drink for the sake of Anglo-Kenyan relations. I decided that if it was so important, I could force down one more.

Josephat came and sat down with us, while the guy who turned out to be his right-hand man, collected the drinks from the bar. I was slightly concerned when he put a full crate of White Cap beers on our table, especially as a crate contained 25 bottles. I looked at Peter, and he simply said, 'Yes, the drink he's bought us is a crate of beer.' The right-hand man, who never spoke throughout the evening, opened a bottle for each of us and sat down without one, on the next table. Josephat raised his bottle towards Barry and me, and said, 'Welcome!'

Whenever our beers were almost empty, Josephat's sidekick would jump up and open another bottle. There was clearly no escape. Before I became too fuddled to think at all, I wondered if the British Ambassador in Nairobi would appreciate the lengths to which we were going to maintain good relationships in local communities. It was dark when we eventually staggered out of the bar. It was dark in a way I had never seen at home. When clouds obscure the moon and stars in Britain there is always reflected light from some nearby city or town. There were no lights to reflect in this part of Kenya, and it was pitch black. We were all too drunk to drive the car, but we couldn't walk home because we couldn't see a yard in front of us.

The headlights of the car were our only hope of finding the way back, and as the keys were in my pocket, I was delegated to get us home. There was no chance of anything else being on the road, so I drove very slowly down the middle of the road with one eye closed, because I was seeing double. We got home safely and found Sang, sitting patiently in the dark, waiting to serve a rather over-cooked meal, which we devoured, again for the sake of Anglo-Kenyan relations.

The weather is dry and sunny for most of the year in Kenya, but there is a distinct and reliable rainy season, which lasts about six weeks. We had been assured we would be home before the rainy season started, but this time it came early. The local soil contains a lot of clay, and all the roads are made of local soil. It rained all one night and when we tried to run in the morning, we had to stop after two hundred yards. Every footstep picked up more and more sticky mud until it was impossible to lift our shoes off the ground.

Peter and Shaun thought it might be just a single storm rather than the rainy season, and suggested we wait for it to dry out. It rained for the next three days, and the road became impassable to anything, except maybe a tank. Peter arranged for us to stay with friends of his in Eldoret, where we could run on tarmac, if we could get to Eldoret. On the fourth day the sun was shining and we took this chance to get out, before we became stranded for the rest of the month.

We slithered and slipped along the road, but always managed to keep moving forward. After an hour, we came to a section of road under repair, and for at least a mile, only one side of the road was open. Half way along these road works we met a pick-up truck coming the other way, just as it started to rain. I signalled for them to go backwards and they signalled for me to go backwards. I got out and talked to the driver.

When I got back in the car Barry said, 'We can't back up for half a mile. I hope you've made them back up.'

'They reckon I should reverse into the ditch. Th ey'll drive past, and then stop and push us out.'

'You didn't agree to that, did you?'

'Yes,' I said.

'But they'll just drive straight on, and we'll be stuck in this ditch for a week.'

The edge of the road was severely cambered, and the

bottom of the ditch was full of very wet, sticky mud. I was a bit nervous, but I said, 'No, they won't. It'll be fine.'

I reversed the car onto the edge of the camber, and gravity took over. We gently slithered, at almost 45 degrees, into the bottom of the ditch. The pick-up truck drove past, and, much to our relief, stopped. Four of the six Kenyans got out and, while I drove in second gear, they pushed from the back. They pushed and pushed and we didn't move an inch. They told me to rev harder; then all four of them stood on the back bumper and jumped up and down as hard as they could. We started to move. The front wheels were nearly on the road, the back wheels were in the ditch and for fifty yards we bounced and skidded sideways towards Eldoret. Suddenly we got a bit of traction and we were back on the road. Our helpers jumped off, and I waved my thanks out of the window, not daring to stop.

Barry was giving me a strange look. I told him there had been no need to panic, and I had always been confident they would help us. 'I wasn't thinking about that,' he said. 'I was just thinking how pleased that guy in Nairobi will be that we've looked after his car.'

When the trip was over and we got back to London we went for a five mile spin, but I wasn't laughing at the end of this one, because my Achilles tendon was sore. After a week of jogging and treatment it settled down and I was able to train well. In June I won a 3,000m race in Edinburgh, and then beat a good field over 5,000m in the annual AAA v Loughborough College match. At the end of the month, I went to Crystal Palace for the AAA 5,000m feeling confident that I could make the team for the Commonwealth Games, as this race was the trial. There were a lot of top athletes running, and it was won by Henry Rono, who was probably the best in the world at the time. The pace was just too fast for me and I finished 12th, but more importantly, fourth Englishman. With a maximum of three runners per country, I wouldn't be going to the Games. I was disappointed, but just felt resigned to try again next time.

A month later I trimmed my best to 13 min 37 sec with fourth place in the UK Championships. That run earned me a place in a 5,000 metres race in Warsaw, where I was out-sprinted in the last lap by three Russians, but slashed my time down to 13 min 28.7 sec. It had been a good season with a lot of progress.

The start of 1979 brought several bouts of deep snow, which had me trying to train in multi-storey car parks, and along the middle of the road. I finished 24th in the National Cross Country, and helped Gateshead to another team title. A couple of weeks later I won the Windermere to Kendal 10 mile road race, but had to walk home after a few miles of the next day's run because my right tendon was so sore. On April 11th I was back in the Taplow Hospital listening to Dr Williams' classical music and trying to lie very still, as he cut all the scar tissue away from my tendon, under local anaesthetic.

I went through the full course of rehabilitation at Farnham Park and was discharged from there a day before my 27th birthday. I began the long process of building up my training. I had been through this before, but this time I continued to have problems. The tendon was a little sore and lumpy, and the bottom of the scar pulled when I started to run. I got physiotherapy and persevered, but by mid June I was back seeing Dr Williams. He thought the pain was caused by an adhesion and gave me a small anti-inflammatory injection of methyl prednisolone, after which I had to rest for 48 hours.

I got back into steady running but never felt confident enough to run on the track or attempt anything very fast, because it never felt totally right. I was back to see him again in August, and he thought I had bursitis, for which he recommended short-wave physiotherapy treatment. While having treatment,

I was able to work my way up to 70 miles a week and ran some reasonable road races, but the soreness kept coming back and I saw Dr Williams again in October. By now he must have been sick of the sight of me and said there was nothing more he could do for me, but he referred me to an orthopaedic specialist.

I continued to run between 70 and 90 miles per week, but the tendon would hurt for the first few miles and then feel ok. It used to hurt every morning getting out of bed, but would get better after walking around for a while. This constant niggle was wearing me down and sapping my confidence, but I also had other important things on my mind.

I was working in my father's business, but he was still very much running it. I had come into it with the intention of taking over from him, but the years were slipping by, and I still wanted to concentrate on my sport. He never put any pressure on me at all, and always said that this was his way of helping me to run, but he was in his sixties and I was still more interested in running than the total commitment that ownership of a community pharmacy brings. I asked him what he would do if I didn't want the business, and he said he would sell up and retire. I had suspected this, and now knew that I was taking advantage of him, so I told him to sell and I would do locum work. Within six weeks of this conversation, his pharmacy was sold and he was retired.

Although my father had helped me a great deal, it was always difficult trying to run twice a day, work five and a half days a week and have a social life. I never let anything stop me from training, but I was always very good at fitting it in to keep some balance in my life. If I was going out for the whole day on a Sunday, I would get up at 6:30am, run 15 miles and have the whole day free by 9:00am. It was never a question of either or with me; it was always a matter of how I could fit them both in.

Around the time my dad sold his business, I met the

lovely daughter of a local farmer. We had been out together about three times when we both had a day off work, and I suggested a day trip to the Lake District. By mid afternoon we had stopped in Grasmere. She said she had an old friend living there, and would like to visit her. I said I would leave her to catch up with her friend, and come back in about 40 minutes. Being the thoughtful, considerate woman that she was, she asked what I was going to do. Naturally, I was going for a run.

To allay the fears she had for the rest of the journey, I showed her the contents of my boot. I had a kit bag of running gear, a large plastic washing up bowl, a bar of soap, a sponge, two large vacuum flasks of hot water, a couple of towels and some deodorant. I changed in the car, ran five miles, and had a full body sponge bath out of the boot of the car. It may come as no surprise to you that I haven't seen her for a lot of years, but I have heard through the grapevine that she still tells the story of the strange man who took her on a date, and went for a five mile run in the middle of it.

It was in December 1979 that I went back down to Taplow and saw a podiatrist, who said I was in a vicious circle of pain and running awkwardly to avoid it. I was over-pronating and needed an orthotic device to correct the movement of my foot over the ground. This may sound commonplace now, but in 1979 podiatry was a very new science, and this was radical stuff. He took a plaster cast of my foot and made a customised orthotic out of cork and leather. In 1979 cork and leather were the materials of choice in this cutting edge technology.

After a week of running with this new device in my shoe, I had a large and deep pressure blister on the arch of my foot. When this settled down, I was able to do a few months of consistent training with nothing more than an occasional twinge. This was the year of the Moscow Olympics, and I was running 80 miles or more every week in my bid to make the

71

team. I finished 5th in the UK Championship 10,000m, and went to Edinburgh for the Olympic 5,000m trial hoping to do just a little better. There were 32 runners, which made it a difficult race to run. With five laps to go, I worked my way up to a good position within a few yards of the leaders, but when the pace quickened, I couldn't respond. Barry Smith came third and won his place on the Olympic team, but I finished 13th in 13 min 57 sec and another season had finished in disappointment.

Eight years had gone by since I ran 4 min 4 sec for a mile. I had managed a few decent times, a handful of minor international races, and a third place in the AAA Championships. Despite nearly a decade of evidence to the contrary, I believed I was capable of more, but success seemed so elusive.

CHAPTER 6

THE BEER DRINKER'S GUIDE TO SPORTS PSYCHOLOGY

I was living in Durham and one day, when my car was out of action, I went to Newcastle on the train. On the way back I was late and rushed into the station just as my train left. I had an hour to wait until the next one, but rather than be annoyed, I decided to make the most of it. My running was finished for the day, so I went to the pub. I like pubs and I like beer; I always have done and I expect I always will. There are some grand, old pubs near the station and within a couple of minutes I was ordering a pint of real ale.

I really enjoy the great flavour and variety of traditional beer. Some people complain that you sometimes get a pint that is poor quality, but I don't worry about that because sometimes you get one that is tremendous. I find that keg beers and lagers are always the same wherever you go. They are reliable but average. They can never soar to the heights that real ale can reach at its peak. As I sat down at a small table in the corner, my first sip confirmed that I had just bought a masterpiece in a glass.

One of the places I had been to in Newcastle was a bookshop. I had bought a couple of novels, a notepad, and a copy of the Concise Oxford Dictionary. I pulled the notepad and a pen out of my bag and laid them on the table. I felt like I needed to make a plan. I had committed myself to running when I walked away from my father's business, but I didn't seem to know how I was going to fulfil whatever potential I had. All I had done was burn my bridges, and I felt unsure about how to make progress. I needed to do something different, but I didn't know what.

I picked up my pen and wrote, 'What do I want?' at the top of the page. I started to make a list of things like 'improve my times' and 'win more races', but I soon realised that I had been trying to do those things for the past ten years.

I needed to look at things differently, and I remembered an article I had read about a company that wanted to recruit a new employee. They advertised the job in various newspapers. They gave a full description of the work involved and offered a salary of £60,000. They got no response; nobody applied. They were surprised, but decided to re-advertise the job a few weeks later. They ran exactly the same advert in the same newspapers, but changed the salary to £25,000. This time they got dozens of replies. The article went on to talk about the self-image that everybody has, and how it is shaped and reinforced by all the experiences in our lives. This self-image affects everything we do. It determines the way we dress, where we live, the car we drive, the friends we have, the job we do and the salary we earn. The people applying for the job had never imagined they were worth £60,000, but could see themselves earning £25,000. It is very difficult to cross the boundaries of the map we all have tucked away in our heads, because our subconscious minds always want to guide us to somewhere familiar and safe. Our accumulated experience tells us who and what we are, and our minds make us act in a way that fits our own particular comfort zone.

I tried to imagine how somebody could do a job for £25,000 but couldn't do it for more than twice as much. But then I thought about what it would be like for very shy people, who are asked to give a presentation to a big audience. They would start to sweat, breathe harder and their pulse would quicken and they might feel nauseous. These are strong physical reactions caused by the prospect of leaving the comfort zone.

For years I had assumed that my failure to run better was down to a combination of injuries and not training hard enough; but I started to wonder if it was my own self-image that was holding me back. If making a presentation could create such a strong physical reaction, then surely the prospect of winning a big race could cause a reaction that was strong enough to make sure I didn't win. Perhaps 'running quite well but not winning' was exactly what my subconscious self-image thought I should be doing.

This idea came as a shock, but I quickly realised that it was probably true. I used to be the boy in glasses at the bottom of the class who couldn't kick a ball and came last in a handicap race. I had to retake my A levels to get into the polytechnic. Perhaps I had turned down my father's business because I didn't think I was worthy of it. Why would my self-image involve great achievements? Apart from a couple of decent races, I had never done anything to suggest I was going to be better than average.

I consoled myself with a mouthful of beer, and kept the delicious flavour in my mouth while I wondered what to do. Eventually I decided to swallow it and I began to smile. Whenever I have a problem, I always feel better about it when I know what's happening. In the same way that I felt better in hospital when I realised I was having a life-threatening anaphylactic shock, I now felt better because there was a plausible reason for my level of performance. In hospital I hadn't worried too much about how my body was going to survive the trauma it was going through, and now I wasn't worrying too much about how I was going to change 28 years of uninspiring, accumulated experience. I was simply happy that I was going to try to do it.

I picked up my pen and wrote 'change my mind'. Realising what this usually meant I wrote, 'I am not going to change my mind about this; I am going to alter my mind'. The question, of course, was how? As I was wondering where on earth to start the process of changing my subconscious self-image, the man at the next table was joined by a younger man.

'Hello Thomas,' said the older man, 'Where's Paul?'

'He's at the bar getting some drinks,' said Thomas.

'So, how are you?'

'Not bad,' replied Thomas.

'What did you think of my proposal?'

'Yeah, not bad. I think it'll be a lot of work, and there is no guarantee, but it might succeed.'

A third man came to the table with some drinks, and the older man greeted him.

'Hello Paul. How are you?'

'Fantastic,' said Paul. 'I loved your proposal. If we do the work for it, it could really succeed.'

I had no idea what they were talking about, but I felt sure that Paul was going to do a better job than Thomas. I stopped listening, and thought about my reaction. They had only said a few words, but from those words I had concluded that one was going to be more successful than the other. I was intrigued. I knew nothing about their talents, experience or ability, but from the words they used, I could tell a lot about their attitude. Thomas wasn't looking forward to all the work involved, especially as there was no guarantee of success, whereas Paul didn't seem worried about the work because it might bring success. I realised how similar this was to a running career. There was no guarantee of success after years and years of training, but the work had to be done to provide the chance of success.

I was suddenly struck by an interesting thought. I had intuitively decided that Paul would do a better job than Thomas after hearing them both speak for a few seconds. I had gone some way to explaining it when I analysed it, but my opinion had been formed instantly. I started to wonder if my own subconscious mind was intuitively expecting a lack of success for me because of my attitude. To most people my attitude would have seemed good; I trained twice a day come rain or shine; I had come back many times from serious injuries, and I had even given up the opportunity of my father's business to pursue my sport. But I was starting to realise that although I had an attitude that made me diligent in my training, it wasn't the same thing as having an attitude that would make me successful in my running. It was a very small word that made me realise the difference.

Thomas was probably very diligent in his work, but when asked how he was, had replied, 'not bad'. I realised that whenever I was asked how I was, or how my running was going, I also said 'not bad'. I took my new dictionary out of its bag and opened it at the back. There were 1,358 pages of word definitions. I flicked my thumb across all the pages until I got to aardvark, and wondered how many thousands of words had just flashed before my eyes. I had bought the dictionary because I like to learn new words, and I sometimes need to cheat in crosswords, but mostly because I enjoy language. English is a wonderfully diverse and expressive language. When used effectively, it can be incredibly descriptive, moving, uplifting, poetic, inspirational and eloquent. Yet despite all this, when asked how my running was going, the word I chose to use was 'bad'. I qualified it by putting 'not' in front of it, but out of all the thousands of possible words, I was selecting 'bad' to describe my favourite activity.

I tried to justify myself by thinking how everybody tends to say 'not bad' and it's just a custom and doesn't really mean very much. I stopped because I suddenly knew how wrong my attitude was. I wanted to be a successful runner, and to be successful I had to be a lot better than average. Most people are average, and I had to be different to most people if I was going to be better. Doing or saying something because most people did it wasn't going to help me to be better than them. I needed to do, say and think things in a better and different way.

Paul had answered the question about how he was in a better way than anybody I had heard before. He had said 'fantastic'. His attitude to his work was good, and he felt fantastic about himself. I really liked the sound of this. I felt as if I was starting to grasp the need for an attitude of success, above and beyond an attitude of mere diligence. I picked up my pen, and under the heading of 'What do I want', I wrote, 'I want to feel fantastic. I want to feel absolutely fantastic'.

I took a few sips of my drink, and started to relish the idea of developing a new successful attitude. I liked the idea that I had to be different to most people, if I was going to become better than average. I really liked the idea that it didn't mean I had to train harder than everybody else, because it was dawning on me that I needed to think differently to everybody else, and by thinking differently, I could develop an attitude of success.

This sounded great; if thinking differently was going to make me a better runner, I could do it sitting in the pub. I smiled to myself and took another drink as I figured I was making myself a better runner right now. A few moments later, I realised that I still hadn't answered the all important question. How was I going to change the attitude I'd had for the last ten years?

I looked around the pub at everybody talking. I looked at

my dictionary, and then at my notepad. I saw the word fantastic, and realised what I had to do. It was simple, but probably not easy. I had to change my vocabulary. I realised that if I changed my vocabulary, I would change the thoughts in my head. When I changed my thoughts, I would change my actions. When I changed my actions, I would get different results.

That seemed quite logical to me, but when I missed all the steps out and wrote down 'improve my vocabulary = run faster' I thought it sounded crazy. But then I remembered that I had already decided to think differently to most people, so I wrote 'think differently' as a heading above it, and suddenly it became a legitimate idea.

Having crazy concepts was fine, as long as I could turn them into something practical. Nearly every runner I knew talked about training hard, and how much harder they were going to train to get better. I had often felt this attitude was a problem for them and already had some ideas about it. I began to wonder how I could take a different approach, and a stream of thoughts came into my head.

If I thought I had to train hard, it followed that I would have to train harder and harder to get better. This was true up to a point, but if I went on training harder, I would become too tired, stale and probably injured. It was true that my performance would improve with more training until I reached the optimum level, and beyond that point, more training would make me worse.

If I thought in terms of training hard, I was in danger of never being satisfied. Even if I had done some excellent training I could always tell myself I could have done more, or I could have run quicker. What I really needed was to train to my optimum level; to do enough but not more. Enough for a top runner is a huge amount of physical work, but if I thought in terms of optimum training, I was sure I would be happy and satisfied with what I had done. The problem with this was the word itself. People like to say 'I train hard' because they can put so much feeling and emotion into it, but you just can't say 'I train optimally' with passion in your voice. The concept was right, but the word was no help. I just couldn't feel excited about training optimally. I needed a different word.

I started to think about all the group track sessions I had done when somebody had run the last one or two efforts faster than the others. If we were doing, say, 10 times 400 metres in 66 seconds, there would be someone running the last one or two in 64, because they wanted to prove to themselves that they could do more or go faster. I figured there were two main problems with this. First, they were given a set of instructions or a target, which they decided to change at the last minute. Surely this teaches the subconscious mind that whatever you set out to do isn't good enough, and that your intentions are unreliable. Secondly, they are left feeling dissatisfied, because having run 64 for the last repetition, they then wonder if they could have run 63 if they had tried harder. The whole concept of training harder can make you feel like you should have done more, no matter how much you have done.

I compared this with running all 10 repetitions in the required 66 seconds. I would have achieved exactly what I set out to do, and could feel satisfied with a job well done. My subconscious would learn that when I complete the task I set myself, it feels good. If I could have run faster at the end, I could look forward to doing a better training session next time.

I knew I had to think about optimal training, and avoid the concept of hard training, but what was I going to call it? Suddenly, I realised that getting ten out of ten wasn't optimal, it was perfect. That was the word I needed, and from now on I would try to do 'perfect' training. Every time I achieved what I set out to do, I was going to call it perfect. If I did my 10

80

repetitions in 66 and the guy training with me left me behind on the last two, that's great, because my training was perfect, but his was hard.

I imagined that every time I told myself my training was perfect, my subconscious mind would store it. Eventually it would become used to being perfect. Every time the other guy said his training was hard, his subconscious would store it and learn to expect running to be hard. When it came to the big race, the really big one, he would be thinking, 'this race is going to be really hard; I will have to run harder than ever.' His subconscious would know that running hard was never good enough, and to make reality fit with this self-created image, it would make sure that he ran a race that just wasn't quite good enough.

But if I could get this right, when I thought about the big race I would say to myself, 'this is a huge test for me, it will be very difficult, in fact, to do well I will have to run the perfect race.' To this my subconscious mind would respond, 'the perfect race? No problem, I do that all the time.'

I had read various things about positive thinking, and some people said you could do anything with positive thinking. I didn't agree with that. No matter how positive my thinking was I would never be a sprinter or high jumper, because I didn't have the fast twitch muscle fibres to do it. I decided that you can't do anything with positive thinking, but you can probably do everything better than you would with negative thinking. But what I was trying to develop wasn't positive thinking, it was specific thinking. Like using the right words, I wanted to think in a precise way that would make me more successful.

The obvious question popped into my head. What precisely did I mean by successful? I knew that I wanted to be successful, but I was shocked to realise that I had never really defined it. I thought about times, victories, medals and championships, but struggled to identify a performance that I could call a success because I didn't know what I was capable of achieving. Everything I thought of was an unknown; it might be too ambitious, it might not. I didn't want to define success as something I may not be able to do. I decided that success was becoming the best I could be, whatever that was. I wanted to get better and better until I couldn't improve any more.

I wrote on my pad, 'Success is measured by how much I fulfil the talent I was born with.' I liked this because everybody could use the same definition of success, and therefore I felt it had to be true. I also felt as if my inadequate self image was going to like it because this definition meant that I no longer had to compare myself with other people. From now on, all I had to do was compare the new me with the old me. If I was improving, I was becoming more successful, and if I kept the process going I was ....It hit me. If I kept it going until I truly fulfilled whatever talent I had, I couldn't be more successful. Nobody could be more successful. I may not win the prizes and acclaim of someone with more talent, but I could be just as successful as them. This was the sort of thinking I was looking for. I realised that when I eventually retired from running, I would know how much I had fulfilled my talent, and that whatever level of success I reached, it was entirely down to me.

I felt good, but knew that I had to continue developing a precise plan. Reaching my ultimate success would be a journey of many stages. I had to set more goals. I had to keep asking myself 'what do I want?' on a short term, medium term and long term basis. My long term goal was to be the best I could be, but I was in a competitive, measured sport and I had to achieve some clearly defined steps. It would be crazy to set off on a journey without knowing the route. I picked up my pen and three times I underlined the words 'what do I want?'

Self doubt was never too far away with me, and as soon

as I had put my pen down another question popped into my head. Why? Why did I want these things? As I thought about it, I realised this wasn't self doubt; it was to eliminate doubt. If I really wanted something I should know why I wanted it. If I couldn't answer the question why, then perhaps I didn't really want it. I tried to imagine running some race because my club or a coach or my family thought I should, and coming to the crunch moment when I felt as if I was flat out, but I had to find a little bit more. How much could I find if other people had put me there, compared to how I would respond if I was desperate to win for my own reasons? I felt sure that 'why do I want it?' was just as important as 'what do I want?' so I wrote it down and underlined it.

These two questions led inevitably to a third. How much do I want it? That crunch moment in a race would be altered by why I was doing it, but it could be transformed by how much I wanted it. I suddenly remembered a story I had heard many years ago. A little boy was playing in the garden, while his mother was busy inside the house. Suddenly she heard a terrible screeching noise, a thud and then silence. She looked out of the window, but the boy wasn't there. She ran into the garden, but he wasn't there. She ran to the street and in the middle of the road was a car with the driver sitting paralysed by shock. Under the wheels of the car, her little boy lay motionless. There was nobody else in the street, and the driver was still in shock, so she ran to the car and tried to pull the boy free, but he was trapped. Filled with fear and dread, she grabbed hold of the side of the car and with a huge effort lifted it up; she arched her back against it and with a free hand pulled the boy to safety.

I have no idea if this story is true, but I decided that I was going to believe it. I don't know what car levitation translates into as a running performance, but I loved the idea that in very special circumstances someone could produce a feat of physical strength that would be completely beyond them in a normal situation. A mother's desire to protect her child is a very powerful instinct, and running was never going to be a matter of life and death, but the prospect of being able to run better than ever before, by dint of my desire to do it, was thrilling.

As I was writing 'how much do I want it?' on my pad, I was distracted by more people joining the group nearby. They were now a chair short at their table and to one of the newcomers, Thomas, said, "You could ask Einstein in the corner if he can spare that stool." As I happily let the guy have a seat I wasn't using, I realised how incongruous I probably looked. I was surrounded by people talking to each other, while I sat by myself at a table with a dictionary and a notepad on it, staring at nothing for most of the time, and occasionally making a note. My immediate reaction was to be irritated by his sarcasm, but then I remembered that he was the one with the attitude I was trying to lose. I was sitting here trying to think differently to him, so I changed it round, and inside my head I pretended I was with someone (she was very beautiful as far as I remember) and, silently, I said to her, 'See that guy over there? He compares me to Einstein. But, of course, he's wrong. Einstein was a very clever guy, but I am pretty sure that over 10K I could have thrashed him.' (As far as I remember, she was impressed.) I decided that thinking and doing things differently to the average person was necessary to be better than average, but it would sometimes make me stand out as different. The way to deal with this was to embrace it, have fun with it and try to enjoy it. I also decided to develop the ability to switch things round in my head, so that when I was faced with a problem I didn't react to it, but instead I responded to it by finding something positive and useful in it.

The mention of Einstein made me remember something he once said, which was 'imagination is more important than knowledge.' It seemed an odd thing for such a knowledgeable man to say, but he meant that knowledge is an accumulation of what is already known; however, to discover new things you needed to imagine what they might be and how you might find them. I imagined if it was good enough for Einstein, it was good enough for me.

I was sure that it was almost impossible to achieve a performance that my mind, or self image, thought was beyond me. So perhaps I had to imagine myself as a better runner before I could become one. I wasn't thinking about the sort of world beating fantasy that most runners have when they are running through the park. I was thinking about precise, mental rehearsal that would lead to better results. I would train my mind to accept the reality of the performances I imagined.

As I savoured another sip of my drink, I felt as if I needed one more piece to complete the jigsaw. I needed something different, something special. I needed some inspiration. I tried to imagine myself as various famous runners from the past, but that didn't work because it didn't fit my definition of success, which was all about my success from my talent. I needed to use my imagination more.

Perhaps I could use something from the animal kingdom? The cheetah was the fastest runner on earth. The lion was regarded as the king of the jungle, and the eagle was magnificent as it soared high up in the air. I couldn't identify with any of these because their special qualities came naturally to them, and my self image didn't include any innate greatness. I needed something more humble. I let my imagination wander and eventually I found what I needed at the bottom of my own garden.

This is a very humble creature indeed. It doesn't look inspiring, it doesn't sound inspiring, but when my imagination realised what it thinks it became truly inspiring to me. I felt sure that I now had what I needed to succeed, and on my pad I wrote

'I am going to think like a caterpillar.' The caterpillar spends its time surviving. It hides from birds and eats leaves, but it is one of the most ambitious creatures on the planet because all the time it is thinking, 'one day I am going to grow beautiful wings and I am going to fly.'

If my self image could not relate to a cheetah or lion, surely it could be as ambitious as a tiny twig-like creature at the bottom of my garden. The caterpillar needs both time and the right conditions to fulfil the incredible potential that is hidden inside it. Perhaps I could be just like the caterpillar, and with my new approach I could discover potential inside me that had never yet been seen. If I could feed my self image with caterpillar thinking and get all the other conditions just right, perhaps I could fly free from my comfort zone and, one day, travel all the way to the fulfilment of my talent.

I turned the page on my notepad and wrote a summary of everything I had decided. 'Change my vocabulary. Aim for perfection. Know what I want, why I want it, and how much I want it. Use my imagination. Try to feel fantastic, and think like a caterpillar.' I was sure my self image would have no trouble identifying with such a lowly creature, but would it be able to transform when the time came? If I kept saying to myself 'one day I will do this and one day I will do that' I had to realise that eventually the day would come when I had to say 'and today is the day'.

I finished my beer and looked at my watch. I had a decision to make. Should I have another pint of Eureka, or go for the train? This was the new me. I went for the train.

CHAPTER 7

BOSTON

I was 28 years old, and knew that I had only a few years left in which to display the ability that I believed lay hidden inside me. After a decade of quite good performances, I realised that I would have to do something drastic if I was going to start producing really good performances.

I had recently taken a big decision about leaving my dad's business. A more sensible man would have balanced my lack of real success in running against the opportunity to take on a lucrative and safe business, which would have provided me with a decent life style, along with the respect of the local community, which my father enjoyed. But then a sensible man wouldn't be involved in a sport which involved training twice a day, for years, with no guarantee of success and very little hope of ever making any money.

I didn't rush into this decision, but I knew I had to make a change. What did I want? I wanted to be the best I could be. I wanted to finish my running career feeling that I had fulfilled myself. Why did I want it? I wanted to avoid having some perpetual nagging doubt about what I might have done if only I had kept trying for a little longer. It was a deep, personal desire to see what I could do. How much did I want it? I had already given up the chance of my father's business, so I knew I was ready to make whatever changes to my life that I thought would help me.

I knew I had to do something different to get different results; so I resigned from my job, sold my car, rented out my house and moved to Boston, Massachusetts. I chose Boston because I knew people there from a previous visit, and it was the base for many of the top American distance runners, including Bill Rodgers and Greg Meyer. Being there would be a fresh start to my running career; I would have great facilities, lots of competition, plenty of training partners and perhaps new influences and ideas.

All of the above is entirely true, but it's not the whole story, because there was also a woman involved. I had met her in England; I had been to Boston to see her; and she had been back to England to see me. She was the real cause of the demise of my relationship with the farmer's daughter, rather than my oppotunistic training runs.

Many years earlier my dad, in his wisdom, had told me never to worry too much about relationships, because women were like buses; if you missed one there would be another one along in twenty minutes. My father had grown up in an age when buses ran on time, whereas people from my generation know that when it comes to buses, you wait ages for one and then two come along at once.

I had given up my job to pursue my running career, not to pursue this woman, but having decided to make a completely fresh start to my sport, it made a lot of sense to go to the top-class running centre where she lived. Or, at least, it would have made a lot of sense if, just two weeks before I got there, she hadn't met the man she later married.

My fresh start had turned sour on the day I arrived, but

people I had met on my previous trip helped me out. Henry Finch was a runner and architect, who, with his friend Roger, had bought a large, rundown house in the Boston suburb of Waban. They were updating and improving it as they lived in it, along with several rent paying house mates. I lived with them for a couple of weeks until I found somewhere permanent. Henry showed me several of the best local running routes, and introduced me to a friend with a sports shop, where I was able to do some part time work.

One of Henry's house mates was Mattie Parker whose sister was looking for someone to rent a spare room in her house. After an interview over a beer at the kitchen table, I was accepted and spent the rest of the year in nearby Auburndale with Anne Parker, her demented dog, and a vegan called Sheila, who was in the depths of an unrequited love affair with Jackson Browne. Well, she had every one of his records.

I knew I had to do something different, and this was very different to living in Ferryhill. What was not so different was the discomfort in my left Achilles tendon, which restricted me to running a couple of miles a day for the first three weeks. I had arrived in Boston at the end of September 1980, and it took till November to work my way up to a pain-free 65 miles per week. In mid-November, I entered a local 10K road race, which in England would have been known as the Newton 10K, but there it was billed as the Great American Smokeout 10K at Heartbreak Hill. The course was basically up and down the 'Heartbreak Hill' section of the Boston Marathon, and if there was any irony in me running my first race there, I am pleased to say that I was able to ignore it.

Henry Finch came with me, and as I warmed up he checked who was running. Apparently, the only real opposition was Vinnie Fleming. I had heard of him, and read about him in race reports, but Henry wasn't the slightest bit worried and reckoned I could easily beat him. I was glad Henry was there because he had the supreme level of confidence in my ability that I should have had, but didn't.

I began the race steadily, and ignored the usual charge from the start line. Fleming soon developed a gap at the front, and after about a mile I picked up my pace to catch him. He must have thought the race was already in the bag because I still remember the look on his face as I caught him. It was only an expression but it definitely said, 'who on earth are you in your multi-coloured T-shirt catching me after I've already pulled clear?'

I don't know what his expression was as I moved away from him at 2 miles, but I do know that mine was a very large smile when I finished the race a minute and a half clear in 29:16. Winning is always good, but winning my first race over there was especially important. A year earlier, I had run the Heaton Road Race in Newcastle, and finished two seconds away from the course record. It sounds good but it didn't feel good because I am referring to the course record when the race started. I finished a distant third, a minute behind Barry Smith and Mike McLeod. Barry and Mike both went on to be Olympic athletes on the track, but I didn't know that at the time, and if I had it probably wouldn't have made me feel any better about being thrashed in a local road race. I am sure I didn't run any better than that in the Great American Smokeout, but winning certainly made me feel better.

I didn't have to run for a club in Boston, but I liked club membership for the sense of community and belonging it brought. Many of the best runners in the area were members of the Greater Boston Track Club, but I didn't know any of them, other than by reputation. I had been receiving shoe and clothing sponsorship from Nike for a couple of years, and continued to do so in the States. Nike had their own running club, called

Athletics West, but this was only open to Americans. My third option was Henry Finch's club, Cambridge Sports Union, which I joined because Henry had helped me, and because they had lots of social events, which is what I really meant by a sense of community and belonging.

The third Th ursday in November every year is Thanksgiving. It is an important holiday in America, when families get together and eat a traditional meal of roast turkey. A week after my first race, I was competing again in the Cambridge Sports Union Turkey Trot. It was a five mile race involving two laps of the perimeter of Fresh Pond. It was a very easy event for the club to organise because there was a five mile race every Saturday at Fresh Pond. The only organisation required was for the social afterwards.

'Fresh Pond' is a great institution in Boston. At 10 o'clock every Saturday you can turn up and get a race over one lap (two and a half miles) or keep going for two laps (five miles). There are no entry fees and no prizes, but the first five men and women get their name in the sports section of Sunday's *Boston Globe*. On a cold but sunny day, I went through the first lap in 11:25, and slowed slightly on the second lap to fi nish fi rst in 23:06, which was a time I was very happy with. A week later, I was racing again in the Braintree 10K road race. My confidence had improved and I set off hard. I was clear after a mile and beat Dick Mahoney, by quarter of a mile, in 29 minutes on a hilly course. I had run three races in three weeks and won them all. I had never done anything so confidence boosting in England.

I was very pleased with my performances and my housemates were very pleased with the television set I won as fi rst prize at Braintree. In this current age of millionaire sportsmen, a television may not sound like a big deal, but for me in 1980 it was. My status in Myrtle Avenue, Auburndale climbed considerably when Anne and Sheila realised that all this running I kept doing could have tangible benefits.

Winter was on its way, and winter in Boston is severe with deep snowfalls and exceptional cold. After a sudden fall of four inches, Henry showed me one of his solutions to impossible running conditions, and we did five miles round and round the basement corridors of a large office building. A week later, he showed me a considerably more prestigious indoor facility. Harvard University's indoor track is not the sort of place that is open to the general public, but Henry knew the guy on the door and got us in. I had never been on an indoor track before, because there was only one in Britain and it was in Birmingham. This was one of four in Boston, and it was probably the best surface I ever ran on. At half the size of an outdoor track, it had banked bends and an outdoor track's synthetic surface, laid on beautifully sprung wooden boards. The tension, or spring, in the underlying boards was set by a group of scientists after extensive research into the mechanics of human movement. It felt like they had got it right as Henry and I ran 10 by 200 meters in about 30 seconds. A week later, I was running 10 x 400m in 61 seconds, while the snow piled up outside. I couldn't possibly have done that sort of session in December, in the cold, damp wind at home.

I used to think winters were cold in North East England until I went to Boston and discovered what cold really is. Each day I had to check the temperature before I ran, and dress accordingly. I had a variety of layers I would wear depending on how many degrees below freezing it was. The coldest temperature I ran in was 4 degrees Fahrenheit, which is minus 15 degrees Centigrade. The radio and television gave out warnings advising people not to go outside unless it was absolutely necessary. I deemed it necessary to run fifteen miles that day, but heeding the warning, I wore the three layer kit of full length thermal underwear, a fleece running suit, a nylon windbreaker suit, thick gloves and a woollen hat pulled down over my ears, with Vaseline smeared on my lips.

When it was that cold it was usually a cloudless sky, and the sun shone brightly. Snow was piled high on the side of the road but the road was completely dry. I would have enjoyed running on days like that if not for the effect extreme cold had on my nose. These temperatures irritate the nasal cavities, and to protect the membranes from damage the nose produces copious amounts of secretions. I had a moustache at the time. My only excuse being, so did a lot of other people. The secretions would run down into my moustache and freeze, and as I ran further, this iceberg of frozen snot on my top lip would grow bigger and bigger. Luckily, because of the weather warning, there was hardly anybody out to see it.

Mattie and Anne Parker were going to spend Christmas with their mother and kindly invited me to join them. She lived in a small town somewhere in New Jersey, and we drove for hours and hours on Christmas Eve, arriving at her house well after dark. On Christmas Day I got up early so that I could do my run but not interfere with anybody's enjoyment of the day. It was minus 14 Centigrade but with a wind that made it feel much colder. I felt cold even with the full three layer kit on.

When I run somewhere I have never been before, I set off in one direction and keep going straight until it is time to turn round and retrace my steps, and I have always been able to find my way back. After nearly 40 minutes of running on this freezing Christmas morning, I had reached another small town and had to stop for the traffic before I could cross the main street. As I waited, a car with a family in it pulled up, wound down the window, and asked me how to get to Lake Street. They drove away again very quickly after I put my ice covered face in their window and said, 'I don't have the faintest idea where I am, never mind where you are going.'

On the day after Christmas, I caught a bus back to Boston because I was racing on the 27th. I ran 8 minutes 12 seconds for 3,000 meters on a flat indoor track and won by 2 seconds. I had now raced four times and won them all. None of my performances had been exceptional, but there is nothing like winning races to build self confidence, and self confidence is essential to make the progression to better performances. I was also enjoying life in Boston. People there are very proud of its historic buildings. I have to say that having grown up close to Durham Cathedral, I found it hard to go "wow" to a 200 year old Town Hall, but it is an attractive city to a European eye and it has a great deal going on. I particularly enjoyed a number of bars with regular live music, by some very good local bands.

I was making friends and meeting a lot of new people through Henry's housemates and the running club. A lot of single, working people shared large houses, and they all had their own circle of friends. When a house had a party, which was often, they could invite a lot of people, and everybody's circle of acquaintances grew rapidly. I enjoyed these parties because they weren't 'bring a bottle' parties; they were 'bring a plate' parties. Everybody brought something to eat, so there was a fantastic spread of food, but nobody had to go to too much trouble or expense. They worked best if there was a little bit of organisation though, because you didn't want everybody to turn up with a bowl of guacamole.

I suffered my first defeat on this trip at the Dartmouth Relays meeting in Hanover, New Hampshire, over 5,000m. This was a much higher level of competition, and I was happy with my run. The 220 yard track had no banking on the bends, and after leading with 440 yards to go, I was out-sprinted by a Kenyan, called Chebor, and Matt Centrowitz, who won the American 5,000m title on four occasions. I ran 13:59 and beat some good runners like Ray Treacy. I was very pleased to break

14 minutes in the middle of January. I was running 85 miles each week, with one session of fast pace on an indoor track, and that one session a week was obviously making a big difference.

After beating some of the Boston based members of Athletics West at Dartmouth, I was invited to train with them by their coach Bob Sevene. I ran a few times with John Flora at the Boston University indoor track, and a typical session was 2 sets of 2 by half a mile in 2 min 15secs, and a mile in 4 min 30secs. The halves were fairly comfortable, but keeping the same pace going for a mile made it tough. Having a training partner of equal ability helped me enormously in this sort of workout.

At the end of January I ran 5,000m at The New England Indoor Championships, at what felt like my home track of Harvard University. It was a talented field, but the clear favourite was Greg Meyer. He was a prolific winner of road races, but also had a sub four minute mile to his name. He went straight to the front and I tucked in behind him. We went through the first mile in 4 min 23sec, and the two of us were clear. He glanced behind, and hoping that meant he was feeling the pace, I went past him. A couple of laps later he passed me, and then I retook the lead as we went past two miles in 8:51.

This was the regional championship and there was a big crowd inside the building. They were making a huge amount of noise, because they loved watching two men fighting each other for the lead. With half a mile to run, I was just about to make a big attack, when Meyer surged. He got a couple of yards clear, but because I was ready to go myself I quickly closed it. With two laps left I went past him, and with waves of deafening sound bouncing off the walls, I summoned up a last lap of 29 seconds. If you have paid any attention whilst reading this far, you will already have guessed that Meyer out-sprinted me. With a last lap in 27 seconds, he set a new American indoor record of 13:40.6. I ran what was possibly a British indoor record of

13:42.3. I say possibly because 5,000m was never run indoors in Britain at the time and there don't seem to be any lists.

I had that mixed emotion that comes from the thrill of a good race, the satisfaction of running really well, and the disappointment of losing. It wasn't the first or the last time I experienced that sensation. In fact, two weeks later I was feeling it again, when I ran the Gasparilla 15 kilometre road race in the warmth and sunshine of Tampa, Florida. Greg Meyer had won this race the previous year in an American record of 43 min 40 sec. I went round the course in 43:44, but was soundly beaten into 6th place, as the first five beat the old record and Ric Rojas won in 43:12. I calculated that my run was equivalent to 47:10 for the more familiar distance of 10 miles, and I was happy with that.

I had planned to stay in America for a year, but six months was the longest I could stay on a tourist visa, so I came back to England for a while in February. I ran the National Cross Country Championship on Hampstead Heath, and helped Gateshead Harriers to second place team medals. There is an old saying about 'horses for courses', and this race showed me just how true it is. My style of running is best suited to bouncing off the smooth hard surface of a track or road. The 1981 'National' consisted of nine miles of unrelenting deep sticky mud, and I slid and slipped my way to 56th place, five minutes behind the winner, Julian Goater. A couple of weeks later I ran a 10 mile road race and was beaten, yet again, by Barry Smith and Mike McLeod.

As I made my way back to Boston in late March, I realised that if I had stayed in England, I would have had a winter of defeats to Barry and Mike; the biggest race of the season would have been a thrashing in the 'National'; and I would not have been able to do any of my better quality sessions on the cold, wet and windy outdoor track at Gateshead. Another winter like that would not have made me a better runner. I knew I had made a lot of progress, and I wasn't worried that it had gone completely unnoticed on my trip home. I also realised that we all have a tendency to underrate local people and overrate people from more exotic places. I was always being beaten by a couple of local runners, for the simple reason that, at the time, Barry Smith and Mike McLeod were world class. The people I had read about in Boston, but then beaten, simply weren't as good as those two.

After a few weeks back in Boston, I raced a couple of 10K road races on consecutive weekends, and won them both. It was good to be back! At one of them I won another television, and I have to confess that I risked expulsion from the sport by contravening my amateur status, when I sold it to help to pay the rent. I had become friends with Greg Meyer, and his friend Tim Donovan, and the three of us trained together quite often. I blame Greg's influence for my reckless approach to my amateur status, as he was a founder member of the Association of Road Racing Athletes. The purpose of ARRA was to campaign for the right to win prize money in road races. The sport was popular, good events were attracting a lot of fee-paying runners, the sponsors were getting fabulous publicity, but the top performers were getting domestic, electrical goods.

Of course, the very best runners had been receiving under-the-table payments from race organisers for years, because they brought the crowds and publicity to an event. In the amateur system, runners were always under threat from the authorities, and I have heard an unconfirmed story that Ron Clarke, during his record breaking tours of Europe, would never take money for running. Instead, he used to bet the promoter whatever his fee was, that he couldn't do something like jump over a box of matches. When he achieved the feat, he could tell the authorities that none of the money going into his bank account was from running, because it had all been won gambling, which is a much more honourable thing for an amateur gentleman to do.

When the sport first took shape in the 1880s, they had separate amateur and professional codes. There were only a few professionals and they made their money by challenging another professional to a head to head contest, in either a single race or a series. When the Modern Olympics began in 1896, there was a new, worldwide and entirely amateur platform for testing the best runners, and professionalism faded away. Nearly a century later, in the 1980s, few people wanted a return to separate groups; they wanted an open and honest sport where athletes were free to make money, if they were good enough to do it, as they did in other sports.

The authorities were forced to change, but they did so step by step. New rules created the halfway house of Trust Funds, which meant you could win money, but you couldn't spend it. All your income from sport had to go into a Trust Fund until you retired from the sport, and so, if you had never actually received any money for competing, you could still be regarded as an amateur. They still disliked the idea of prize money, so it was referred to as 'participation money at the finish line', and if you got a fee for running, it was called 'participation money at the start line'.

As soon as these Funds were formed, people began to test them. 'Can I use the money in my fund for essential travel expenses?' Yes, you can. 'Well, I need a new car to drive to the track.' 'Can I invest the money in my fund?' Yes, you can. 'I would like to invest it in property. I am buying a new house.'

After a few years, the sport's governing bodies realised they had done what all politically minded people tend to do: they had created an enormous layer of bureaucracy which served no useful purpose. Eventually, the funds were scrapped and the sport became open. However, it didn't affect me at this stage because I wasn't winning any money.

My frequent success in road races around Boston had lead several people to suggest that I should move up to the marathon, especially as my lack of a sprint finish was unlikely to matter over 26 miles. (Little did they know.) I was sure the marathon would suit me, but I needed to discuss such a big decision with Lindsay Dunn. This was long before email, and trans-Atlantic phone calls were expensive, so I wrote him a letter. A week or two later his reply made his opinion very clear. He thought I had not fulfilled my potential on the track, and if I moved up to the marathon, I probably never would. I needed to achieve three things: improve my times; run for Great Britain in a major championship; and win a national title. If I achieved all of that, I would have a running career to be satisfied with, and I could then try the marathon with a lot more confidence.

Lindsay had given me the opposite advice to everybody else, but that never bothered him because he enjoys disagreeing with people. His advice was specific and goal orientated. I had never really thought of winning a national title on the track, because I couldn't win a local road race in Newcastle, and I was invariably out-sprinted at the end of track races. Lindsay was telling me that he thought I could do these things and should, at least, give them a try.

This was a big decision. I suspect I was considering the marathon because I thought it might bring me some instant success, but I soon realised that I didn't want instant success. I wanted to fulfill my ability. I thought I would make a good marathon runner, but I wanted to be as successful as possible, and that meant being the best track runner my talent would allow, before moving up to the marathon. I began to embrace Lindsay's three ideas and develop them into my new goals. I also realised that if I was going to achieve these new goals, I would really have to develop my caterpillar thinking.

The track season was beginning and I planned a series of races which would culminate in the National Championships. My first race was 5,000m in Knoxville, Tennessee. I led for a while but faded badly over the last three laps to finish 12th. Next I ran 1,500m in Boston and came second, and then I ran the New England Championship 10,000m and finished second to Greg Meyer. A week later I flew to Sacramento, California, for the most important race of my season - the American Championship 10,000 metres. All the other races had been building up to this and I felt as if I was going to run well. The opposition was going to be tough, but so were the conditions. The race was held at night to avoid the heat of the day, which was good planning. It had been 100 degrees Fahrenheit (38 Centigrade) during the day, but by race time it had cooled down to 98F or 37C. This was the first time I had ever seen a drinks table set out for a track race, and there was even a man with a hosepipe who would spray you with water, if you raised your hand as you went past him.

I had never raced in heat like this before, and perhaps never been in heat like this before, so I asked Bob Sevene how to approach it. He said, "Joan Benoit won the women's 10K last night and she was sitting in the stand until 5 minutes before the start. You don't need to warm up, you need to cool down." I would normally run about two miles of warm up before a track race, but I cut it down to 400 yards, and then put my head under a running tap. Nobody wanted to go fast, and the first half went by in a fairly comfortable 14:35. Alberto Salazar, who was American record holder at both 5,000m and 10,000m, picked up the pace in the second half and I responded by moving quickly through from 10th to 4th. As he kept the pressure on, a group of five pulled clear of the rest. Another surge from Salazar, with six laps to go, broke up the group and gave him a winning lead. Duncan McDonald, the previous American record holder at 5,000m, was second. I hung on through what seemed a very long last mile to finish third, ahead of Mark Nenow, who went on to become the holder of the World Best at 10,000m on the road.

On the journey back to Boston, I gave a lot of thought to how I had managed to win a medal in the American Championship. Lindsay's letter about making high and specific goals for the track had helped me to focus, specifically on the Sacramento race, throughout my unimpressive build up. I had learnt that I could run really well in my goal race, without having to run really well beforehand. The motivation generated by my goal was more important to me than the self-confidence of great preparation. I also realised that making the drastic move from home to America had my sub-conscious mind thinking, 'he really means it'. I had become committed; truly committed in a way that many runners never grasp.

The track season was over by mid June, and the top American athletes headed for the European circuit, which lasts much longer. In the States, the attention switched to road racing, and on Independence Day I ran the Peachtree Road Race in Atlanta, Georgia. I have distant relatives in Atlanta, because my father's mother's uncle moved there when he was a young man. He wasn't any kind of pioneer; he left England to escape from some scandal or other. I met some of his descendents the night before the race, and decided it was best not to mention the scandal. Thanks to their generous hospitality, they fed me the largest steak I have ever seen. Through politeness I ate it all, and when the race started at 8 o'clock the next morning, I felt as if I had a lead weight in my stomach.

The Peach Tree is a10 kilometre race over a hilly course, with 25,000 runners. I went through the first two miles in 9 minutes, which is around 28:00 pace for 10K. I was about 30th. I couldn't believe that 30 people were going to run that fast, on this course, in this heat, so I told myself that a lot of them would have to slow down, and tried to ignore the fact that I was going to have to slow down. By halfway I started passing people, and for the next three miles I kept pushing on by always having someone to aim at and overtake. World Cross Country Champion, Craig Virgin, won the race, and I worked my way through to 9th with 28:43, which was a personal best for 10K on the road.

It was a month to my next race, and I spent the time doing some good training with Greg Meyer and Tim Donovan. One day Tim came round to my house and said he was on his way to see his friend, Mr Hill, over at the Pump House, and would I like to join him. The Pump House Hill was a favourite venue of theirs. It was on a traffic free access road to a water pumping station, surrounded by dense woodland. It started on a medium incline, slackened off, turned a corner and became very steep, turned another corner and eased off to the top. It took a minute and a half to race up it. We would do six or eight repetitions with a jog back down, and it was here that I learnt to improve my hill running technique. I had never been good at hill running and I was struggling to keep up with Greg on the steepest section until I copied him and took shorter, faster strides. Reducing stride length to run faster doesn't seem logical but it works on steep hills. It must be something to do with the biomechanical efficiency of lever action; I don't know. But I do know I was happy to stay with him, because he loved to hammer up that hill.

In early August I went to Glens Falls, New York, to run The Athletic Congress 15K road race championship. TAC was the governing body of athletics in America, so this was the official national championship, as the Sacramento race had been. All the best runners were obviously unimpressed by this, because none of them ran. The opposition consisted of good up-and-coming young runners and good, older runners at the end of their careers. The top runners were saving themselves for events which offered more tangible rewards than a medal and a TAC title, but with two national championship bronze medals to my name, I regarded a title of any sort as a step forward

I was feeling confident, and went with all the crazy, adrenaline junkies who run the first mile far too fast. By two miles I was a hundred yards clear and held that gap to the finish. I won it in 44:19. I had absolutely no illusions about where I ranked as a 15,000 metre runner in America, but it was important to me, because if I never did anything else in my career, I had a national title to my name.

If I had had any illusions, they would have been shattered seven days later, when I ran the Falmouth Road Race in Cape Cod. Falmouth is one of America's most famous road races. It is seven miles along the Atlantic coast from Woods Hole to Falmouth, and everybody runs it. Even Mike McLeod had come over from England for it. The start was furious, and I couldn't get anywhere near the front, but these weren't crazy guys; these were Olympic and World Championship medallists. Between one mile and six miles I passed 16 people. I know that because I counted them as a means of concentrating on getting as high up the field as I could. I passed more in the last mile and finished in 9th place. It was won by Salazar from Rod Dixon, and Mike McLeod. Craig Virgin was 5th and I was seven seconds behind 6th placed Herb Lindsay, and one place in front of Ric Rojas, the winner of the Gasparilla 15K. I had mixed emotions afterwards. I didn't like coming ninth, but I knew I had run well against top class opposition. I wanted to be a better runner than I was. I knew I had made a lot of progress, but I still had the same desire to improve further. Coming to America had been the right thing to do, and if I continued to do the right things, I was sure I could take another step forward.

To the amazement of one or two runners I knew, I decided the right thing to do was to have a rest after Falmouth, and for the next week I didn't run a step. I eased myself back into it with 44 miles the following week, and then, feeling fresh and eager, I got back to training properly. There are some runners who think that years of training will completely disappear if you have a week off. It is not true. Two weeks after my rest, I ran the Saucony 10K in Boston, and won it in 29:14.

By October my visa had expired, and I had to return to England. I'd had a wonderful time in Boston, and made a lot of friends. I didn't want to leave, but knew that I had to, because there was no long term future for me there. I couldn't work as a pharmacist because they didn't accept my qualifications, and I knew that I needed to go home.

A couple of days after getting back to England, I went for a drink with a group of the guys from Gateshead Harriers to tell them about my time in America. The conversation got round to running shoes, which, at the time, were being developed from very basic trainers to the specialised and technical footwear we have now. American companies were doing all the innovation, and thanks to the people I had met, and my time in the sports shop, I appeared to know more about the right shoe for the right person than any of the others. Brendan Foster was there, and he had just been appointed to set up a division of Nike in the UK. As we left the pub, he offered me a job as a promotions manager in the new company. I hadn't missed pharmacy during my year away, and as it probably wouldn't miss me for a while, I accepted.

A few days later, I was in France for the Paris-Versailles race. It is a 17 kilometre road race from the Eiffel Tower to the Palace of Versailles, and attracts thousands of runners. The first few miles are along the side of the Seine, and I was in a large leading group, which included Radhouane Bouster and Michel

Jeffray from France, and Emiel Puttemans from Belgium. After a couple of flat miles, we turned left up a steep incline of fifty yards. The road turned right and we had another 100 yards of the same incline. We turned left again and the climb kept going to a roundabout. We took the second exit and I could see the crest of the hill sixty yards away, but after fifty yards we turned off this road and up another steep hill to a corner. How much longer could this go on? Around the corner we faced another 100 yards of climbing, and the leading group had whittled down to five. This was an extremely long, hard climb, but I was doing alright because, thanks to the Pump House, Mr Hill was now my friend.

My legs were stinging, but guessing that everybody else felt the same, I lengthened my stride and pushed the pace as soon as we reached the top. Immediately it was down to Jeffray, Bouster and me. In all the races I had won in America, I had done so by surging clear in mid race. As we ran through the forest on the top of the hill, I surged twice more, but couldn't get away.

What goes up must come down, and the loss of all that height was just as steep as the climb. There are two ways to run downhill; you can lean back and use your legs as brakes, or you can lean forward a little and let gravity pull you down. The latter involves long, fast strides, and if you really let go, it can be scarily fast. Jeffray and I went for this option and Bouster was dropped. After a mile or so of running shoulder to shoulder, we came to a short, sharp incline; I worked hard up it, surged harder over the top and started to pull clear. I went on to be a very tired, but very happy winner.

This race wasn't the quality of something like Falmouth, but it was a big event with international European runners. On the way home, I thought a lot about Lindsay Dunn's letter and my commitment to those three new goals. It was the European

Championship in nine months time, and my victory in Paris made me believe that I could compete at that level. All I had to do was get into the British team.

Winning a cross-country race at school.

Being dragged to a personal best for 2 miles (8:26:8) by Tony Simmons (7), Ian Stewart (5), Brendan Foster, Nick Rose (15), and Ray Smedley at Meadowbank Stadium, Edinburgh, 1976. Quadruple Olympic Champion Lasse Virén (1) is next.

Leading in the Loughrea Road Race, County Galway, in 1978. Just about to be outsprinted by three of the best 'kickers' in the world. From left, Eamonn Coghlan, Mike McLeod and Seb Coe.

On the way to winning
AAA 10,000m in 1983.

Passing Ingrid Kristiansen in the London Marathon, 1984.

Just seconds behind John Treacy in the Los Angeles Olympic
marathon, 1984.

With my father and mother, and Olympic medal, after landing at
Newcastle airport from Los Angeles.

CHAPTER 8

ATHENS AND BRISBANE

In 1982 the European Championships were to be held in Athens during September, and the Commonwealth Games were in Brisbane four weeks later. My various road race victories had given me the confidence to believe I might make the team for one of these. I was determined to train as well as possible, to make this dream come true.

Winter training, for most runners, consisted of lots of miles, with occasional cross country races. I knew from my experience in Boston that I needed to include some faster running every week, and without an indoor track, it was going to be difficult. I could do sessions on the track at Gateshead, or, if I had to, I could use a quiet road. Or so I thought.

My training diaries, which record the details of every training session throughout my career, also perform another task. They prove the advance of global warming! It is several years now since snow lay on the ground in Newcastle for more than a few hours, but my diaries record regular falls of lasting snow. In January 1982 we had several inches which lasted more than a week. The track at Gateshead was closed, and all the roads were covered in ice or slush. Easy running was treacherous, and fast running was impossible. I tried training in a multi-storey car park but there were too many sharp bends. I discovered that there was really only one suitable venue in the North East.

The Tyne Tunnel is a well known and extremely busy road under the River Tyne, in between Newcastle and the coast. Half a mile away is the less well known pedestrian Tyne Tunnel, which is about the same width and height as an underground train tunnel. It is best described as dank, but completely free from snow and wind, and it was in this tunnel, beneath the river Tyne, that I tried to replicate the training sessions I had performed on Harvard's award winning indoor track a year earlier. I trained there on several occasions, and rarely saw anybody else travelling through the tunnel. However, I did have a slight altercation with the guard who mans the entrance. Halfway through my first session, he came along the tunnel and told me that whatever I was doing he didn't think I should be doing it in his tunnel. I referred him to the notice at the entrance, which laid down the rules for users of the tunnel. I pointed out that I was clearly a pedestrian; I was not riding a bicycle; I was not smoking or drinking; and, even if I say so myself, I was quite confident that I was not loitering. I always laugh when people try to tell me there is just no glamour in long distance running.

At the beginning of the year I made a detailed plan of my training and racing, up to the AAA Championship in July, which was the trial race for the European and Commonwealth Games. I showed it to Lindsay and we discussed it at length. There were two important things he wanted to change. He felt I needed to do a specific, six week spell of high mileage at 110 miles per week before the track season, and he didn't think I should run a 10,000 metre race before the trial, in case it took too much out of me. At the end of our talk I agreed to change my training, but disagreed about the race. I wanted to achieve the qualifying time before the trial, so I could concentrate on getting in the first three, and not have to worry about the time as well. As our relationship was one of friend and adviser, rather than coach and athlete, we agreed to disagree.

Before these decisions became important, I was back in the USA. I had been invited back to a couple of the races I had done well in the previous year. I ran the New England Indoor 5,000m at Boston University's track. I had surprised myself in last year's event by how quickly I ran. This time I was surprised by how quickly everybody else ran. I went through the first mile in 4:21 and two miles in 8:48, but I couldn't hold it. Instead of finishing fast, I was slowing down and I ran the last 800m in 2:16. I finished 6th in 13:53. John Flora, my previous training partner on this track, had the honour this year of being out sprinted by Greg Meyer, who won by one second in 13:36. I was a little disappointed with my run, but it was probably to be expected. 13:53 wasn't too bad in January, but it was more of a Tyne Tunnel performance than a Harvard performance.

Next on the agenda was a return to Tampa, Florida and the Gasparilla 15k, where previously I had finished 6th in 43:44. This year I managed to improve both my time and position. I was 5th in 43:38. It was hot and very humid. The leading group of four got away from me after passing two miles in 9:01, and I ran most of the race by myself. Mike Musyoki won it in 43:08; with Greg Meyer second in 43:11. This was a good run, and I was very pleased with it. Despite the problems of training in the snow, I knew my winter work was on course.

My job at Nike was working out quite well. My task was to increase exposure of the brand, which I achieved by signing good runners to exclusive Nike contracts. Most of them were glad to sign for the provision of free kit and shoes. Everybody was happy. Nike was getting plenty of authentic advertising, the runners were getting free kit, and I had a job which allowed me to run and race when I wanted to. The downside was that it often involved a lot of travelling, and my training diaries state, without any explanation, that one day I ran 7 miles in Manchester, and 10 miles the next day in Sheffield.

After five weeks of decent training, it was time for my six week spell of 110 miles per week. I started with a 19 mile run with Lindsay, Pete Parker and Steve Winter. It was mid March, and although there was no snow, it was very windy. I felt tired, and continued to feel tired all day. I woke the next day with a severe headache, and felt really ill. I felt so bad that I didn't run a step for the next four days. My first week of high mileage ended with a grand total of 28. I decided to ignore that week and start again.

This time I was alright, and apart from a couple of days with a sore leg, which reduced the fourth week to 86 miles, I achieved my 110 mile target for the other five weeks. I did it, but it wasn't easy. I felt tired all of the time, and I often felt as if I was doing the second run of the day having just finished the first one. I had regularly run 80 to 90 miles per week without any problem, but the extra 20 miles on top had me feeling as if I was constantly out running. However, I felt good about completing it, and I knew it had improved my endurance, so I could move on to the next part of the plan, which was altitude training.

Boulder, Colorado was, and still is, a favourite place for runners. It is 5,000 feet above sea level, which is high enough to have an altitude stimulus, but not so high as to make quality running impossible. If you stand in Boulder and face east, you can see flat farm land disappearing into the distance. If you turn and face west, you have to look up to see the snow covered peaks of the Rocky Mountains.

In late May, Lindsay Dunn, Barry Smith and I went to Boulder for two and a half weeks of training. Conventional wisdom says that this is too short a period of time for altitude training to provide a benefit. I discuss this idea in a later chapter, so for now, I will just say that conventional wisdom is not always right.

Barry and I had done lots of endurance work, and the purpose of this trip was to propel our cardiovascular fitness forward so that we could race well on the track, and hopefully both make the British team. When you run at high altitude you have to make concessions to the rarefied air, but a lot of people seem to do this by running more slowly. We had come to run fast, so all our steady runs were shorter than usual but a little quicker too. One of the track sessions was 8 x 440 yards - they didn't have a metric track - in an average of 62.7 seconds, but with three minutes jog between efforts instead of the 90 seconds I would have taken at home. The extra rest didn't make this session any easier; it just made it possible.

I also did one of Lindsay's infamous 'unknown' sessions, where I had to run every effort at 62 seconds per lap pace, but I didn't know what was coming until I jogged up to the line and he called out the distance I had to run. I also didn't know how many reps I was going to do, and he always made me jog up to the line ready to go again before he told me I had finished. I won't repeat what I usually called him.

He still likes to tell the story of one of his sessions I did later that year. It involved running at a predetermined pace whenever he blew a whistle, and keeping it going until he blew it again. I was well into the session, and had just done a long effort, when, after only forty yards of jogging, I heard the whistle and set off again. I was cursing him for giving me so little rest and, as I came into the home straight, I couldn't understand why he was laughing. It turned out that the whistle I had heard was from a football game outside the stadium. Afterwards, when I had recovered, I laughed about it too, but I also realised that the ability to surge, when very tired, could prove extremely useful.

After ten days in Boulder, we went into the Rockies to a

place called Snowmass, which is at 8,500 feet. Barry and Lindsay stayed, but after two days I went back to Boulder, because I found it impossible to run at anything faster than a jog. I felt this sort of altitude was too much and it wasn't doing me any good.

The day before we came home I ran a session of 3 x ¾ of a mile in 3 minutes 22 seconds each. This is about 28 minute pace for 10,000m, which was the pace at which I was hoping to race. The comment in my diary next to this session is 'excruciating; oxygen debt was huge'. Perhaps the race would be easier, but there again, perhaps not.

After a week at home, I ran a local track league 1,500m in 3:50.1, and ten days later went to Oslo for the Bislett Games 10,000m. This was the race Lindsay had thought I should miss, but I wanted to run it for the European championship qualifying time of 28:30. There was a top class field, which I was lucky to be in, and though 10,000m is 25 laps of the track, I let the leaders go during lap one. It wasn't really a race for me other than against the clock. For a long way I ran in isolation near the back, but after passing 5,000m in exactly 14 minutes, I started to overtake people who had gone with the pace and blown up. Carlos Lopes defeated Alberto Salazar in a new European record of 27:24, which was only two seconds away from Henry Rono's world record. I avoided being lapped by finishing eighth in 28:17, which was a big personal best and comfortably inside the qualifying time.

There were about twenty or thirty British athletes at the Bislett Games. People like Steve Ovett, Seb Coe and Dave Moorcroft could run anywhere because every meeting wanted them, but the rest of us were there thanks to Andy Norman. Over the previous few years he had gained control over what happened in British athletics, thanks to his dominant personality and brusque manner. He wasn't easy to get along with, but getting along with him was a good idea. At meetings like the Bislett Games in Oslo, he worked closely with the organisers, and guaranteed that the big stars like Coe and Ovett would run, but in return he wanted twenty other British athletes to be given places in the meeting. This was a huge help to people like me. I would never have got a place in this race without being part of Andy Norman's package of athletes, and these events gave me, and others like me, fantastic experience of top level racing in a packed stadium.

Of course, he made it very clear that a poor performance was not acceptable, and anybody who failed to run well could forget about ever asking him again for a race abroad. I knew I had been outclassed by some of the best runners in the world, but I was pleased with knocking nearly 30 seconds off my personal best. When he saw me after the race he said, 'Spedding. Did you get lapped?' I said, 'No, I didn't.' With a kind of sneer he said, 'It must have been close' and walked off. Over the next few years, as I got more used to him, I began to realise that if he said anything to you that didn't compare your performance to excrement, it was his obtuse way of giving you a compliment. It just never sounded like a compliment.

A week after Bislett I ran an invitation mile at Steve Cram's local track at Monckton in Jarrow. I don't really know how I managed it but I finished last in 4:25, which is only slightly faster pace than I had just run for six miles. I was shocked to perform so badly, but realised that my mind simply wasn't on it. The AAA Championship and trial was getting close and this race just didn't mean enough to me. However, it did shake me up enough to run a personal best for 800m in the local track league four days later. A lifetime best of 1 minute 56.7 seconds for 800m shows quite clearly why I needed to run the longer distances!

I assume that Andy Norman hadn't seen the result of

my mile in Jarrow, because a week before the AAAs I was picked to run 5,000m for England, at Crystal Palace, in a four sided international against Japan, Spain and Kenya. I also assume that a lot of the faster 5,000m runners had turned it down because it was too close to the trial, but I was glad of the international vest and the race.

This international vest, however, was actually a bit of a hassle. Nike was sponsoring the England team, and it was part of my job to make sure the team kit arrived on time, and in the right sizes, which ranged from small to extra, extra, extra large. Everything was fine, but it involved dealing with Andy Norman and a strict deadline, which was far from stress free.

I had learnt the hard way that going too fast in the first few laps of a 5,000m always had me in trouble later. The early pace in this race was quick so I settled in at the back, but this had me in a different kind of trouble. Andy Norman was on the infield, and started barking at me to pull myself together, get my finger out and move up. I ignored him. A few laps later, the pace at the front slackened and then I moved up until I was in third place. With six laps to go Koskie, one of the Kenyans, surged and I went with him. We were soon clear of the rest, and we ran together until 450m to go, when I sprinted hard, and stole a gap on him, which I kept until the end. Winning for England, in front of a full house at Crystal Palace, was fabulous. The crowd were on their feet and cheering, and as I jogged a victory lap I had to pass Andy Norman, who paid me the huge compliment of grunting, 'not bad, for the kit boy'.

It had been an evening meeting, so I had stayed at the Queen's Hotel with all the other athletes. At breakfast the next morning, Andy Norman was sitting with three other officials from the Athletics Association. I apologised for interrupting his breakfast but I wanted to be sure about the selection policy. He confirmed that the first three Britons in the AAA

10,000m would be picked for the European, and the first three Englishmen would be picked for the Commonwealth Games. To be absolutely certain, I asked, 'So, if an Englishman is in the first three next week he is in both teams?' 'Yes,' said Andy Norman. I went back to my table but I wasn't out of earshot when they all had a bit of a laugh after one of them said, 'I can't imagine why he needs to know that.'

I was a little upset by his coment, but, on reflection, had to agree that he probably had a valid point. My best of 28:17 looked very average compared to the recent times of others in the trial such as Julian Goater (27:34); Mike McLoed (27:39); Geoff Smith (27:43); Bernie Ford (27:43); Adrian Royle (27:47); Nick Rose (27:50); Dave Clarke (27:55), Barry Smith (28:06) and Steve Jones, who had just run 13:18 for 5,000 metres.

The trial was back at Crystal Palace and there were plenty of other British runners, along with the Japanese and Kenyans, who had stayed from the previous week. The Norwegians were also using the race as their trial for the European championships, which meant that 45 runners went to the start line. It was crowded and awkward during the first few miles, but despite so many runners, nobody wanted to push the pace. We reached 5,000m in 14:20. I felt comfortable, but I assumed that most of the others were comfortable too.

I started to move closer to the front, because someone was bound to push on at some stage, and I didn't want to miss the break. With six and a half laps to go, I was in about 8th place when I saw Goater surge to the front. The moment I saw him move I surged too. It was a reflex, as if I had heard a whistle. I was almost sprinting down the back straight passing people who hadn't responded so quickly. By the home straight I was third, with Steve Jones in second. I knew this was the decisive moment, and no matter how hard it was, I had to get with Jones and hang on.

Goater ran the next lap in 63.4 seconds and I was just about holding the gap to ten yards. When he ran 66.9 for the next one, Jones and I were able to close up and form a group of three. It was really hard but I knew there was a decent gap behind me and if I could hang on I would be in the team. The next lap was 66.3 and our leading group was still together. Goater wasn't thinking about the team, he was thinking about winning, and he pushed the pace down to 64.5 for the next lap. There were a couple of yards between Goater and Jones and a couple more to me. When he ran 62.9 for the penultimate lap, he was away.

I was incredibly tired now, but I concentrated totally on staying within a couple of yards of Jones, and finished 2 ¼ seconds behind him in third, with 28:11.00. Nick Rose was fourth in 28:17. I had run the second 5,000m in 13:51. Goater ran the second half in 13:43 for a winning time of 28:02. When I got my breath back, I was ecstatic. I had run another personal best; I was going to Athens and Brisbane; and with a bit of luck I would bump into those guys from the breakfast table.

I had made no plans beyond the trial, because making the team was my only plan. I always found that it helped to have nothing planned beyond the target race, because it focused the mind so well. When things got hard, I couldn't start thinking about an alternative if there was no alternative. But now I had six weeks to wait for the European Championships, and ten weeks for the Commonwealth Games, and I felt as if I had already peaked. I discussed this with Lindsay, and we agreed to go back to a little more mileage, with fewer quality sessions, to try to maintain my fitness without pushing it over the edge. We also agreed that our conversation at the beginning of the year had worked out well, because I had ended up with the right decisions on the high mileage training and racing the Oslo 10,000m for the qualifying time.

During the period before Athens I raced with typical

irregularity. I ran a good 13:29.1 for 5,000m in Koblenz, but also managed to take a pedestrian 2:01 to run 800m in Sunderland. Neither performance mattered very much, compared to how I would run in the Championships. When we got to Athens we were expecting to run heats on Monday and a final (if we made it) on Thursday, but the organisers decided there weren't enough runners to justify two rounds, and they altered it to a straight final on the Monday. Some people weren't happy about the last minute change, but I always try to see everything in a positive light, and I regarded this is as good news – I was in the final without having to exert myself.

It was a hot evening in Athens in early September, and as you would expect in a European final, there were a lot of fast runners. I was very nervous about running a major championship, and I always find it curious that I was so nervous, I was almost dreading something that I had spent years longing to do. I knew there was no chance of getting a medal, and I went to the start line not knowing what I was aiming for. I simply had to run the best race I could.

The first 5,000m passed in an uneventful 14:05, and I was happy to stay in contention for as long as possible. With nine laps to go, Carlos Lopes surged to the front with a series of laps in 64 to 65 seconds. As he made his move I was behind Alex Hagelsteens of Belgium, who had run 27:26 when finishing third in the Bislett race. I figured that if I could hang on to him I would do well, but his pace didn't change. I was thinking, 'come on, let's get after them' but he made no response, and I overtook him and gave chase myself. This process only took a couple of seconds but in those seconds a leading group of five had made a gap I couldn't close.

I learnt a vital lesson here about giving an opponent's reputation too much respect. If I had responded instantly to the surge as I had done in the AAA 10,000m, I may have been able to hang on to the leading group long enough to be pulled clear of everybody else. With eight laps to go I was in 6th place, running hard with a gap in front and a gap behind. It was going to be a long two miles to the finish. Steve Jones and Salvatore Antibo of Italy were running together and caught me with three laps to go. They were too good for me round the last lap and I finished eighth in 28:25. I had mixed feelings about it afterwards. Having started the season with a best of 28:45 and no realistic hope of making the team, I should have been delighted with eighth in Europe, but it bothered me that I had made a mistake, and had not been able to hang on to sixth.

When I looked back at this result a few years later, I felt a lot better about it, because the winner, Alberto Cova, went on to win World and Olympic titles; second placed Schildhauer won a few European medals; and third placed Vainio won silver in the '84 Olympics, although he was later disqualified for drug taking. Carlos Lopes (4th) went on to be Olympic marathon champion and record holder; Julian Goater (5th) won a Commonwealth medal later that year; and Antibo (6th) went on to win two European titles and an Olympic silver medal. Steve Jones (7th), who again finished two and a bit seconds ahead of me, went on to win bronze in the World Cross Country and set a World best for the Marathon. It eased the disappointment of finishing eighth to realise there were no mugs among the seven who beat me.

The English team travelled to Australia a week before the Commonwealth Games began. I left home on Saturday morning on the train to London. We flew to Dubai, Kuala Lumpar, Singapore and Sydney, then changed planes and flew to Brisbane, arriving at midday on Monday. I was extremely tired and disorientated, but I recovered and adjusted with a couple of days to spare.

I had travelled to the other side of the world to run this

race, but right next to me on the start line was my arch rival from Tyneside, Mike McLeod. He had made the team because Steve Jones was running for Wales, and Nick Rose was in the 5,000m. The first half of the race went by in a comfortable 14:17. With six laps to go, Goater surged hard, and McLeod and I followed immediately. For a lap England filled the first three places, but I couldn't hold on to this pace, and was passed by Gidamis Shanga and Zack Barie of Tanzania. Those two worked together and caught and passed Goater. With three laps to go I passed McLeod and hung for fourth, in a repeat of the 28:25 I had run in Athens.

I was very pleased with fourth, and delighted with my year. It had been a very long season; I was extremely tired, both physically and mentally, and I barely ran a step for the next three weeks. I took the rare opportunity to enjoy the Gold Coast beaches and relax. I watched the rest of the Games from the stand with a great sense of satisfaction, but on the last day, as we were all standing for a national anthem, I looked around at the crowd and vowed to myself that this was not the end; I would be back for more Championship racing.

The following winter didn't go very well. I was starting to get problems with the arch in my left foot and I had several bouts of viral illness. I was failing to do consistent training, and the few races that I ran were nothing better than average. However, I had a meeting with Lindsay about plans for 1983, and his idea was perfectly simple. After finishing third in the AAA 10,000m last year, surely I had to aim to win it this year. I had improved my times, and I had been to a couple of Championships, so a national title was next on the list. The logical simplicity of his argument had me agreeing straightaway. Having pulled off an unlikely goal last year, I felt more confident that I could pull off an unlikely goal this year. In early January I put a year planner on the wall of my office at Nike and wrote 'AAA 10k' against the

23rd of July. Every morning, for the next six months, I looked at that entry and calmly said to myself, "I am going to win that."

In February, I went to Tampa for the third time to run the Gasparilla 15k. I finished 14th in 44:15, and knew that my interrupted training was to blame for the half minute I had lost on previous runs. The race was won by Rob de Castella in a scintillating 42:46. The winning time for this race was getting faster every year, and I was reminded very clearly that no matter what you had achieved previously, top class performance requires top class training. I managed a couple of weeks at 90 miles before running the National Cross Country. I finished an embarrassing and dismal seventy sixth. I was reminded that top class performance requires a lot of top class training.

I began a six week spell of 110 miles per week straight after the National. I managed it on three out of the six weeks. In the worst week I ran a meagre 49 miles, because I was ill with a temperature over 100 degrees Fahrenheit. However, I had to go to work because the World Cross Country Championships were in Gateshead, and the Nike promotions department had so much work to do in preparation.

After the mileage spell finished, I went to Oslo to run a 10k road race and I struggled the whole way to finish 13th in 29:50. I then did several weeks of 85 miles with some good quality sessions, before my first track race of the year. I ran the North Eastern Championship 1,500m and finished 7th in the heats in 3:59. It was eight months since Brisbane, and I hadn't run a single decent race. However, I was still looking at the entry on my wall chart for July 23rd, and still telling myself that I was going to win.

I had done a session of 3 x 1,200m in 3:12 a few weeks earlier, when Lindsay suggested I do it again but with differential pace. The idea was to practise racing, and I had to run the first lap in 66 seconds, surge the second lap in 61, and deal with the tiredness by running the third lap in 65. I was delighted when I did it almost perfectly, and I soon saw some improvement with a 3,000m in 8:02. In late June I went back to Oslo for the Bislett Games 5,000m, where I ran very close to my best with 13:29.7. I finished 12th, which was fine in such a high quality race, but what concerned me was that, despite beating Geoff Smith and Steve Jones, I was only sixth among the British runners. Eamonn Martin, Dave Clarke, Nick Rose, Julian Goater and Steve Binns all finished ahead of me.

Ten days later I was back on the same track for the Oslo Games 10,000m. It was another world class field and I saw it as a chance to run a really fast time. I went with the leaders from the start, and passed through 5k in 13:45. It was far too fast. As Carlos Lopes went on to win in 27:23, I blew up in spectacular fashion, and struggled to the finish in 28:49. It took me over five minutes to run the last four laps. This was not the ideal way to prepare for a national title attempt.

Every time I ran a track race in Britain the same guys would be there at the check in and we would all warm up together. I liked them well enough but invariably the conversation would be about injuries and illnesses, or about who else was running really well. I always found this type of banter detracted from my concentration on the task ahead. I knew that I had to be totally focused for the AAA Championship, so I planned to avoid all contact with my competitors before the race. Everybody stayed at the Queen's Hotel at the AAA's expense, but I booked myself into another hotel nearby, at my expense. Before the race I nipped into registration, picked up my number and disappeared before anybody could speak to me.

There is a swimming pool at Crystal Palace, which is near the track, and I went to the far side of it to warm up for the race, by myself. I ran up and down the edge of the building repeating a sort of mantra to myself. I jogged to the warm up area just as we were all taken onto the track, and I made it to the start line without anybody having the opportunity to put the slightest negative thought into my head. I knew that I had run only one decent race all year, but it didn't matter. This was going to be my best race of the year, because today was the day, and I was going to fly.

The World Athletics Championships were taking place in Helsinki two weeks after the AAA, and there were a lot of foreign athletes at the meeting. The biggest threat in the 10,000m was the Australian Commonwealth marathon champion, Rob de Castella, who was using this as his last race before the World Marathon. I stayed close to the front throughout the first 5,000m which I passed in a decent 14:08, with de Castella, Geoff Smith and Allister Hutton, who had finished one place behind me in Brisbane.

After 6,000m de Castella went to the front to stop the pace from slacking. On a few occasions he gestured for someone to lead and help him with the pace. I was having a bad spell at this point, and was struggling to stay positive. But even if I had felt good, I would not have led, because I was there to win, not to help him to run a fast time. With six laps to go I snapped out of my bad spell and began to anticipate the finish. We all let de Castella lead, but as we approached the line with three laps to go, I surged to the front. I ran 63 seconds for the next lap.

When you make a long run for home, you have to run fast enough to get a gap but not so fast that you can't hold on. I had certainly gone fast enough to get a gap, but whether I could hold on, only time would tell. I ran 65 seconds for the penultimate lap, and people on the side were telling me that I was still clear. I didn't look round; there was no point - they were definitely chasing me. When I reached the bell I was gasping for breath, my legs were stinging, but I knew I had to pick it up. I ran really hard down the back straight to make sure nobody could get close enough to out sprint me. As I turned into the home straight, half a dozen runners I was about to lap moved out into lane two. I ran for the line as hard as I could, and with fifty yards to go I pulled level with the lapped runners, but I couldn't get past them. I felt as if I was running through treacle. I was clawing at the air trying to pull the line towards to me, and I staggered across it almost drowning in a sea of lactic acid.

I had run 64 seconds for the last lap, and I won in a new personal best of 28:08; Geoff Smith was three seconds back with Allister Hutton third in 28:18; de Castella was fourth in 28:24. As I jogged a very slow victory lap I was reminded of something I had written on a notepad in a pub several years before. What do I want? Why do I want it? How much do I want it?

CHAPTER 9

HOUSTON AND LONDON

National champion at 10,000m I might have been, but a fast finisher I would never be. The Olympic Games in Los Angeles were only eleven months away, and I had to make a major decision. I had a slim chance of making the team at 10,000m but even if I did, I just wasn't quick enough to stand much chance of getting through the heats. I always thought the marathon would suit me, and now was the perfect time to find out, especially as I had fulfilled all three of the targets Lindsay and I had worked on.

The Dublin Marathon was in October, and I decided to run it. The standard was always decent without being world class. I didn't want to run against the very best people in my first one. I just wanted to test the distance and then make a decision afterwards about my plans for Olympic year. I knew that I had to commit myself to one event or the other. Running London as my first marathon, and hoping I could do well enough to get on the team, wasn't the approach that would work for me. I knew that having the alternative of the 10,000m in the back of my mind, as I ran in London, would risk a poor performance. I always needed total commitment and focus to run my best.

Four weeks into my training for Dublin things were not going well. A week after winning the 10,000m I had developed a sore Achilles tendon which lasted for four weeks. The background training I lost through this latest injury was affecting me. I showed Lindsay my training diary, and he confirmed what I already knew: I didn't have enough time to be ready for Dublin, and I would have to find another race to run. I still wanted to run a test marathon, and then make a commitment to either the London Marathon or the 10,000m trials, but time was running out. My first marathon would have to be in January at the latest, or I wouldn't have enough time to recover from that one and prepare for London.

The Houston marathon was the only race in the world which fulfilled my criteria. It was held in mid January, and was won year after year in about 2 hours 12 minutes. I didn't want my first one to be run at 2 hours 9 minutes pace, and 2:12 was a time I thought I could run. If I couldn't run at that sort of pace, I had no future at the distance. I contacted the organisers and told them I was the AAA 10,000m champion, I had been 4th over the same distance in the Commonwealth Games and I was moving up to the marathon. Out of all the races in the world, their race was the one I would like to make my debut in, and could they add me to their list of invited runners. They listened to what I had to say and had no hesitation in saying no.

I tried again through an American agent, who often dealt with the race. He said it was hopeless because they had a rigid policy of paying for runners who had done 2 hours 16 minutes or quicker. With no previous marathon to my name, I didn't qualify. This was the race I had to run, so I spoke to them one more time. Could I run the race if I got myself there? Absolutely. If I got myself to Houston they would meet me at the airport, pay for my hotel room, provide my meals and really look after me.

A return flight from Newcastle via London to Houston was £750 at the end of 1983. This was a big chunk out of my savings, but I bought the ticket and studied the prize money list. There was prize money for the first 15 men, and if I could finish 8th or higher, I would cover the cost of my travel. I believed I could do that.

I had twelve weeks to prepare, which seemed like plenty of time. My Achilles tendon continued to niggle but only occasionally forced me to miss any training. Other things cut into my training. I seemed to have two weeks of good training, then an illness. I'd have two more weeks and then sore calves, which forced me to stop for days. Training in the middle of winter was a lot harder than the middle of summer, and training to the limit always invites viruses and bacteria to take advantage of a stressed body.

When I was problem free, I was training well enough, but I was worried about a lack of consistency. At the beginning of December I ran a 10km road race in London, and finished 9th in 29 minutes 4 seconds. I had hoped to do better, and ran another race in Gateshead two weeks later. The Metro Road Race is about 10km, and as a previous winner and reigning AAA 10km champion, I was expected to do well. I ran the best I could, but the best I could manage was 23rd. People beat me who had never beaten me before. It was the worst road race result I had ever had.

Everyone was asking what was wrong with me. The press wanted to know if I would now scrap my plans to run in Houston. At first I was shocked by my run, but I began to realise it was a symptom of 'marathon madness'. With only four weeks to go, my mind was fixed on my debut over 26 miles, and I had been unable to push myself, because sub-consciously I was holding something back. I told everybody else that I didn't know what was wrong, but I told myself that this was an excellent sign, and it meant that my mind was saving everything for a huge effort in Houston.

During the following week I ran my first over-distance run of 28 miles on December 23rd; 11 miles on Christmas Eve; and two runs totalling 12 miles on Christmas Day. I couldn't let Christmas get in the way of my preparation, but at least all those miles gave me a great appetite. New Year's Eve was also a quiet time, because I ran the Morpeth to Newcastle 14 mile road race on New Year's Day. I finished a well-beaten 6th, and everyone agreed that I was still running as badly as I had at the Metro race. I was unperturbed, and flew to Houston feeling confident that I had trained well. I knew the only race that mattered was this one.

I was met at the airport by John, my designated helper. I was taken to a good hotel and given money for food. John made sure I was comfortable and had whatever I needed. He also showed me some of the highlights of life in Houston, which, for John, included regular visits to a lap-dancing club. I hadn't expected that to be part of my marathon preparation, but it certainly took my mind off the race for a while. However, as the event drew closer, even John's efforts couldn't distract me. I was feeling nervous because I was entering the unknown, but I also felt excited by a new opportunity.

Our start time was 8:30 in the morning. It was unbelievably cold, at a few degrees above freezing, although it was supposed to get warmer as the day went on. I knew I would generate plenty of heat as the race progressed, but to stay warm in the first few miles I had to wear an old pair of socks over my hands and forearms. We had run five miles before I was warm enough to throw them away.

The pre-race favourites were Benji Durden, an American who had won the race previously, and Massimo Magnani of Italy, who had been seventh in the Moscow Olympics. I ran with them, in a large leading group, as we ticked off the early miles in just over 5 minutes each. We passed through ten miles and then halfway without any significant action, and the further we ran, the better I felt. I had expected to run about 2 hours 12 minutes and we were on pace for that.

Magnani needed to win this race to secure his place on the Italian Olympic team for Los Angeles. After 16 miles, he'd had enough of running in this large bunch. He felt that he was the best runner, and he ought to show everyone else it was true. He made his move and accelerated away from the group. It was a fairly rapid change of pace, and only John Wellerding of Iowa went with him.

I wondered if I should be going with him too, but my purpose in this race was to finish in a good time with a solid performance. I was still on course for a time around 2 hours 12 minutes. I was feeling in control, and decided there was no point in risking too much with ten miles to run. I stayed where I was and everybody else in the group ignored the break and carried on as if it had never happened.

After a mile Magnani and Wellerding were out of sight. They had disappeared from view, and we all knew we were running for third place. I began to think of finishing third and how pleased I would be. That would be a great start to my marathon career and it would certainly take care of the airfare with plenty of change left over.

A few more miles ticked by and I felt as if the group was slowing down. I was feeling more and more comfortable. My confidence began to rise as I realised I was certainly going to be able to handle the distance. As we approached 20 miles, I began to plan my own break away.

We reached the 20 mile point and Mark Finucane, from Tennessee, picked up the pace. He and I surged almost simultaneously, and although he pushed very hard, I was with him all the way. After about half a mile we turned a corner. I glanced behind and saw a big gap to the others. He was still hammering along so I told him, it was ok, we were away. He looked at me with a little surprise. I don't know if it was my English accent or the fact that I was talking to him while we were running the hardest mile of the race so far. He slackened off very slightly, and we settled into a good fast rhythm that would take us further away from the guys behind, without us blowing up.

We shared the pace between us and often ran side by side. The last six miles of a marathon is a long way to run hard, but I was thrilled to be going so well. I was thrilled to be secure in either third or fourth place. The road was wide and it meandered its way back to downtown Houston. After about four miles of running together we rounded a corner, and in the distance were the tiny figures of Magnani and Wellerding. We looked at each other in surprise. We hadn't seen them for 45 minutes, and suddenly they were back in sight.

No words were spoken but the looks exchanged between us said, 'Let's get them.' Working together we picked up the pace a little more. Accelerating in the last few miles of a marathon may sound a very difficult thing to do, but the motivation was enormous. Slowly but surely the gap between us was closing. We could see the pressmen on the lead bus, and they must have been able to see us. It was incredibly exciting to be edging closer to the leaders. We were sneaking up on them. In the same way we had forgotten about them when we couldn't see them, they must have forgotten about us and assumed they were having a two-man race.

I kept expecting someone on the press bus to warn them we were getting closer, but they never did. Magnani and Wellerding never knew we were coming until they heard our footsteps ten yards behind them. They looked around in complete shock. We formed a leading group of four just beside the 25 mile mark, and with one mile left to run, it occurred to me that one of this group of four would be the winner. Perhaps it would be me? My thoughts had always been on running a good performance, on seeing if this event would suit me, and on finishing high enough to cover my expenses. Suddenly, with one mile to go, the prospect of winning the race entered my head for the first time.

When you catch people in a distance race, it is usually a good idea to go straight past them, because it doesn't give them time to respond to your faster pace. I had worked so hard to catch the leaders I definitely needed to ease off a little, and gather myself for a big finish. The four of us ran side by side for the next three quarters of a mile. I was very tired but I concentrated on making my move close to the finish.

I had carefully checked out the last half mile before the race began, and I knew there was one right angle turn to come. From the corner it was then 150 yards to the line. With about 400 yards to go Magnani pushed on. I tucked in behind him, and we were all in a line along the road, instead of across it. We were running hard without going flat out. I decided to sprint into and out of the corner, and I hoped this would steal a vital yard or two.

Magnani, of course, had exactly the same idea. I came out of the corner sprinting, but he was sprinting too, and he had stolen a couple of yards on me. The finish line was 150 yards away, and Magnani had a lead of two yards. I was sprinting; trying so hard to pump my weary arms, and lift my aching legs. With 100 yards to go he was one yard ahead of me. I focused on the finish line, and tried to dig deeper for more effort. There was a wall of noise as a loudspeaker bellowed out our names and the crowd cheered us home. With 50 yards to go I was half a yard behind him. The line was coming towards us faster than

I could catch him. I needed more effort. I lunged towards the line. He raised his arms in victory. I was along side him. We were through the finish and I was ahead.

When did I pass him? Was it before or after the line? I didn't know, and neither did anyone else. Everybody was asking who had won. Magnani was certain that he had won, but I wasn't sure. Nobody seemed to know. I was tired and sore, so I walked slowly away and sat down with a drink. People kept asking if I had won, and when I said I didn't know, they couldn't understand why I wasn't more desperate to find out.

Whether I had caught him before the line or not would be announced soon enough, and it was now too late to do anything about it. I didn't show the level of emotion people expected because I was thinking about the answer to my question. Was the marathon going to suit me? Yes, it was. I knew with absolute certainty that I had found my event. The marathon suited me perfectly, and I had really enjoyed it. The result of our close finish was important to me, but not as important as the prospect of a whole new chapter in my running career. A chapter in which I believed I had more chance of success than at any other time. People didn't seem to grasp that I was thrilled about my performance, whether I had won or not.

It was almost fifteen minutes after we had finished before they announced the result. Nobody had photo-finish equipment at the end of a marathon. The officials simply stood on the line and watched what happened. At Houston they had never expected nor experienced a finish so close, and decided to have a meeting before they announced the result. I was lying face down on a physiotherapist's couch, having my legs massaged, when one of the officials found me and told me I had won. There had been no gap between us, but they had all agreed that my torso was in front of Magnani's at the line. We were both given the same time of 2 hours 11 minutes 54 seconds.

Finucane had finished third, just one second behind us.

I had spent my whole running career being out sprinted at the end of races. If only I had known earlier that my opponents needed 26 miles of running in their legs before they were reduced to my sprinting speed. I felt fantastic. My airfare to Houston was the best investment I had ever made, because first place prize money was $20,000, which was a huge amount of money for me at the time.

Massimo Magnani wasn't quite so pleased about the result. He still felt that he had won, and my victory in the last yard cost him $8,000 in prize money, and an automatic place on the Italian Olympic team. Having the same time as the winner wasn't good enough for the Italian Federation; he had to win the race to be picked. He travelled back to Italy knowing he would have to run again in London to impress the selectors.

John took me back to the airport, and persuaded the lady on the check in desk that, as the winner of the Houston Marathon, I ought to be upgraded to first class. As I flew home, sipping champagne, I knew that my run in Houston wasn't quick enough to give me any chance of selection for Los Angeles, but it did give me a lot of confidence to prepare for the London Marathon with the clear aim of getting on the team. I didn't fully appreciate it at the time, but it had also given me the experience I needed to make the very most of my marathon running career. I had chosen to run Houston because it had always had a field of runners with whom I thought I could compete. It proved an excellent decision, because I learnt the most important thing about marathon running, which many runners never give themselves the chance to learn; I learnt how to race the marathon rather than run it. I learnt how to judge my pace; how to make a long, sustained run for home; how to finish strongly; and how it is possible to win from a long way off the pace.

I am always amazed by how many good runners decide to move up to the marathon, and then choose London as their first one, when it is always run at world record pace. Why would anybody move up to a new distance, and guarantee themselves a good thrashing at their first attempt? It's like an amateur boxer turning professional and fighting Joe Calzaghe in their first bout. All you get out of it is a very painful lesson in how you aren't good enough. I don't understand how that sort of experience will ever help a British runner to develop into the sort of runner who can race the marathon and, for example, win a medal in the European Championships.

As a piece of very optimistic forward planning, I had entered the London Marathon and arranged my accommodation before I ran in Houston. There are three types of entry for the London Marathon. Apart from the invited runners, who are proven world-class performers, and the huge throng of fun runners, there is a small group of good British runners who enter the AAA championship to compete for the National marathon title. Before the first London Marathon in 1981, this group of committed club runners and British internationals had run the annual AAA marathon for decades. It used to be held in comparative secrecy, in such exotic locations as Milton Keynes and Sandbach, where the route took runners down country lanes and where the largest crowd was a herd of cows.

I entered the London Marathon by completing my AAA championship entry form and attaching my £5 entry fee. At the same time, I booked a room in a small hotel on the edge of Blackheath Common, less than half a mile from the start line. Using the same approach as the AAA 10,000m the year before, I wanted to avoid all the other runners and immerse myself totally in preparation for my own performance. I needed isolation to focus and concentrate.

The London Marathon was on Sunday May 12th, and I

took the train to Kings Cross on Friday. I didn't want to travel the day before, just in case there were any problems, and also because I wanted a full day in London to focus fully on the task ahead. Saturday was a warm sunny day. I had decided not to run at all, believing that total rest was more beneficial. I would need every scrap of energy on Sunday, and could see no point in wasting any of it the day before. I spent most of the day in my room, watching sport on television. I sat in a chair I had placed directly in front of the set, because I didn't want to watch from the bed in case it gave me a stiff neck.

I have no idea what I watched. It was impossible to be distracted from thoughts of the race. I had always dreamed of running in the Olympic Games, and tomorrow's race was my best, and possibly last, chance to realise that dream. I knew this race would be a defining moment in my whole career. I was very nervous, but I was also very excited. I knew for certain I could run a good marathon, but I didn't know if it would be good enough.

In fact, nobody really knew what was required. The selectors were going to meet the day after London, but they were going to consider all recent British performances. Both Hugh Jones and Geoff Smith had decided not to run in London because they each had a 2:09 marathon to their name, which everyone assumed would be good enough. The only way for me to be confident of making the team was to be the first British runner home.

The day before the race dragged by, but I didn't want to talk to anybody. I needed to stay isolated and focused. Evening eventually came, and I walked to a local Italian restaurant, where I ate lasagne by myself, and overheard people complaining about the roads being closed the following day because of some daft running race.

Back in my room I pinned my race number, 17, to my

white and red Gateshead Harriers running vest, and tried it on, along with my red shorts and Nike racing shoes. I was dressed exactly as I would be in the race, and at last I felt as if I was ready. I stood in front of the mirror, looked myself in the eye and said out loud, 'I'll show them.' I went to bed feeling nervous and woke in the morning feeling nervous, but I slept well all night, which I didn't really understand.

I had one slice of toast and a small glass of water for breakfast. My warm up was five minutes of easy jogging and a couple of quicker strides. The last few minutes before a race begins are crucial. It is easy to become overwhelmed by nerves and self-doubt, and a race can literally be lost just before it begins. I focused all my thoughts on myself, and repeatedly told myself I would run well.

The pre-race favourite was Juma Ikangaa of Tanzania, who had been second in the Commonwealth Games Marathon in Brisbane. He always ran quickly from the start and would be helped by his teammate, Zach Barie. As soon as the race began Ikangaa and Barie were at the front. I had hoped to run in the lead pack, as I had done in Houston, and let the miles roll by, but after only three miles the Africans were pushing the pace well below 5 minutes per mile.

I was confident I could run 2 hours 10 minutes, if I could produce my best. I didn't know if that would be good enough but I was certain there would be very few in front of me if I did it. There was a big group at the front and Ikangaa and Barie didn't like it. They pushed on faster and suddenly I didn't like it. The pace felt too fast for me. I hadn't expected to be making this sort of decision so early in the race, but I checked my watch as we passed the three-mile mark and I was inside 2 hours 10 minutes schedule. I decided to ignore the Africans and run to my watch.

Eighteen other runners thought differently and tried

to stay with the leaders. Over the next half hour the race was split into three sections. There was a small leading group with Ikangaa and Barie dictating the pace; a second group, who had gone with them at three miles but couldn't run that fast; and a third group, where I ran with my training partner and Gateshead teammate, Kevin Forster.

By ten miles both the groups ahead of us were out of sight. Kevin wanted a place in the Olympic team as much as I did, and he was concerned that so many British runners were so far ahead of us that we couldn't see them. We passed 10 miles in 49: 26, which is spot on for 2 hours 10 minutes. I felt great about them all being so far ahead. They had to be running at something like 2 hours 8 minute pace, and the faster they went the more certain I was that we would catch them later. I had learnt in Houston that you don't have to keep them in sight to beat them.

Tower Bridge is one of London's best-known landmarks, and on it there was a huge and noisy crowd of spectators. As we crossed the river I felt happy with my running, excited by the crowd, and ready to push on. The pace in our group seemed to be slowing, as Kevin and I ran side by side along Cable Street to the half way point. We passed through in 65:05. We were pulling away from the third group, and we could now see a line of runners stretching in front of us. Our pace quickened slightly as we closed in on the first straggler. I confess – I felt smug as we swept past him, knowing he had gone too fast and we hadn't. There was another tired runner twenty yards ahead to aim at, then another, and another. We were picking them off like cherries from a tree. It felt good.

After a couple of miles of overtaking people, the gaps became a little harder to close. These guys were running better than the first ones we had caught, but none of them could raise their pace to stay with us. At 16 miles we caught a familiar figure in a blue vest. The last time I had come alongside Massimo Magnani was a frantic blur, but this time we looked each other in the eye. I couldn't resist saying, 'Hi.' He replied with what I presume is the Italian equivalent of 'Ugh.'

A mile later we were edging closer to a group of four runners. Kevin and I realised simultaneously that it was the leaders; Ikangaa and Barie were in front with Oyvind Dahl of Norway and Britain's Adrian Leek just behind them. We pressed on until we were in the group too. It felt wonderful to have caught them after letting them go 14 miles earlier. I knew we had run a sensible, even paced race and they had to be suffering from their early burst of speed.

I didn't realise the significance of this until after the race, but even at this stage, I wasn't thinking about winning. I was still focused and concentrating on running efficiently. My mind was locked into 'run my best performance' mode. When Ikangaa tried to surge away shortly after we caught him, I turned to Kevin and said, 'Let him.' We knew it would be short lived and he would come back to us. He tried several of these surges. We maintained our previous pace, while Ikangaa's surges took care of Leek, Barie and finally Dahl. From 18 miles until nearly 20, it was Juma Ikangaa and two guys from Gateshead Harriers who led the London Marathon.

As we turned into Wapping, Kevin appeared to be weakening, and as Ikangaa drifted back to me after one of his little surges, I accelerated past him. As if a switch had been flicked in my brain, I changed from my passive, 'run efficiently' mentality to an aggressive, competitive 'win the race' attitude. I pushed the pace hard to make sure my move was decisive and, shortly after breaking away, I passed through 20 miles in 1 hour, 38 minutes, 35 seconds. Without looking round I knew I was clear, but I kept pushing on. I wanted to get to the finish line as soon as I could.

The lead vehicle, with the clock and race officials, was just in front of me. Alan Storey, the National Marathon coach, was leaning out of the back shouting at me to 'spread your effort'. He obviously thought I was pushing too hard with six miles to go. I said, 'Ok', but kept running at the same pace.

I was tired and hurting, and the intensity of effort was much greater than before. I reverted to a state of deep concentration. I wasn't thinking about winning, or the Olympic team. I was focused on putting one foot in front of the other as well as I could.

I didn't look round, but Kevin Forster had also passed Ikangaa and was now secure in second place. Past the Tower of London and along the Embankment, I pushed on feeling strong. As I ran through Trafalgar Square I wobbled slightly. The Mall seemed to go on forever, and my tiredness was compounding. Why do they make the last mile of a marathon the longest?

I struggled to run up the slight incline onto Westminster Bridge, but now I could see the finish line, and I knew I had done it. I had set off to run 2 hours 10 minutes and I crossed the line, with my arms in the air, in 2 hours 9 minutes and 57 seconds. Kevin finished a minute and 44 seconds behind. I had won the London Marathon, and I was certain to be picked for the Olympic team. I was too tired to show any outward emotion, but I felt wonderful.

I didn't know it at the time, but as I ran across the cobblestones at the Tower of London, a telephone was ringing in a house in Gateshead. Peter Parker had been Gateshead Harriers club captain for years, until his job took him to southern Ireland in 1983. Although he was away from Gateshead, he remained fanatically keen to follow the sport. He couldn't get television or radio coverage of the marathon at home, and almost two hours into the race he could stand the suspense no longer. He phoned his friend, Archie Hughes, who he knew would be watching, and said,

'Archie, it's Pete. I can't get the marathon here. What's happening?'

'It's great,' said Archie. 'Charlie is in the lead, and Kevin is second.'

To which Pete had replied, 'Stop messing about, Archie. Tell me what's really happening.'

CHAPTER 10

OLYMPIC TRAINING

I had thirteen weeks between London and the Olympic Marathon, and a lot of people were saying this wasn't long enough for anyone to prepare properly. I believed it was. I think people struggle to deal with this sort of timetable because they don't give themselves enough time to recover fully from the first marathon, before training for the second one. I regarded a full recovery as my first priority, and I saw no point in training to the limit again until both my mind and body had recovered from London. I wasn't at all worried about missing training, because I had been in such good condition at London, and all that fitness doesn't completely disappear during a spell of easy running.

I have heard it said that top class runners end up being obsessive compulsives, but I disagree. Top runners have to be determined, focused and committed, but to be really top class you have to be able to make the right decisions under pressure. In fact, I think the ability to make the right decisions under pressure is one of the most important and least appreciated factors in sporting success. Obsessive compulsives often fall short of their potential because, when they are under pressure, they revert to their compulsive behaviour, and make the wrong decisions. I think that taking two weeks to recover from the London Marathon was a correct decision, and one that an obsessive compulsive would have got wrong.

For those who are interested, I have listed all of my training between London and Los Angeles in the appendix to this book, where I also explain the thinking behind it. It took me two weeks before I felt ready to do anything more than easy running, and another two weeks before I got the amount of running up to 100 miles per week. Among all those miles of steady running, there were many sessions of fast running which were all supposed to bring me to a peak of fitness at the Olympics. While each session was part of the whole process, there was one which I felt had a major part in developing my ability to race the marathon, rather than just run it. I learnt about the session from Greg Meyer when I was in Boston, and it involved a 20 mile run with a series of timed efforts throughout it. The first effort lasted five minutes and was followed by a repeating sequence of one, two and four minute efforts. Between every effort there was five minutes of steady running at about 10 miles per hour, or six minutes per mile pace. There was no jogging to recover, so it simulated a series of surges during a race, and the changing duration of the efforts prepared me to cover somebody else's surge, when I didn't know how long that surge would last.

This session was very demanding, and left me feeling tired for the next couple of days. It made me feel slightly nervous beforehand, but I always enjoyed doing it. I loved running, and in this session I got to do a great deal of it. I liked the deep focus and concentration required to stick to the timetable of efforts, but, at the same time, I enjoyed the freedom to run the efforts at a pace that I felt was right. I had to determine, at the time, what pace I could hold for the next two or four minutes, and respond to my body, rather than a pre-determined number on a stopwatch. Racing a marathon sucesssfully is a balancing act between discipline and freedom of expression. This training seesion gave me exactly that, and it always made me feel ready to race those 26 miles.

It is stating the obvious to say that any runner going to the Olympic Games needs to be at peak fitness, and in my imperfect, self-coached world, I felt that my training for the marathon was as close to perfect as I could reasonably expect. I believe I trained with great intensity, without doing too much, but the training I did only tells part of the story of my preparation. I have met a lot of runners who think that if they get the training right, the race will take care of itself. I have never believed that. The training has to be done, but I think you have to make a good race happen, and to do that you have to prepare your mind.

Shortly after London, I planned the training I have documented in the appendix, and I discussed my preparation in general with Lindsay. He reminded me of the AAA 10,000m, where I had beaten Rob de Castella, who had gone on to win the World Marathon Title two weeks later. Lindsay reckoned that I was a better marathon runner than track runner, and if I could beat him over 10,000m, surely I could beat him over the marathon. It was Lindsay who had helped me to set the goals of making the British team, and then winning a national title. Both these things had come true, and so I readily accepted that his latest argument made sense.

There is nothing like setting a stiff goal, which is accomplished, for giving you the confidence to aim for a higher goal. A couple of years earlier, I would have thought it was madness to contemplate beating the world champion at anything, but now I thought of it as logical. Lindsay has since told me that during this conversation he was shocked by how readily I accepted his argument, and when he saw that I truly believed what he was saying, he started to believe it too.

An Olympic medal had always been my very wildest dream; a completely wild dream, because I had been a serious runner for 16 years, and until now I had never been to the Olympic Games. I knew a medal was highly unlikely, but the idea that I could beat de Castella, who was one of the favourites, opened up the idea in my mind that it was possible. I am convinced that the minimum requirement to achieve something is to believe that it is possible.

While that possibility was in the back of my mind, I concentrated on what I could definitely achieve. I had always run well in big races, and this was the biggest race of my life. I was new to the marathon, but it obviously suited me. I felt that whatever happened, I needed to produce the best performance of my life. After a few weeks of thinking like that, I began to believe that I would definitely run the best race of my life. I became totally convinced of it, but to remain convinced I had to get all my preparation right.

The Olympic Marathon is always run in temperatures that are much higher than the ideal. I needed to acclimatise to the heat I would face, so I went back to Boston for six weeks. The British Team were holding their own acclimatisation camp on the west coast at San Diego, but I wanted to go where I knew I would be comfortable, and arranged with the team that I would be in Boston and would make my own way to Los Angeles six days before the race. I knew people in Boston, I knew my way around and I knew where to train. I also knew that it would be about the same temperature as Los Angeles, but more humid, and therefore slightly worse than the conditions expected in the race.

On previous trips to Boston I had made a friend called Steve Toubman. He was going to be touring Europe that summer and said I could stay at his place. He had a room in a small apartment, which he shared with a guy called Andy and his girlfriend. We got along alright for strangers thrown together, and they later told me that as the Games got closer, I became more and more detached. In the last few days before I left, apparently, they would speak to me and I would have no idea that anything had been said. It was as if my entire brain had been taken over by thoughts of the race.

When I flew from Boston to Los Angeles, I was expecting someone from the British team to meet me at the Airport, but there was nobody there, and oddly, there was nothing relating to the Olympics. I knew the Olympic village was at UCLA and I realised I would have to make my own way there. I got a bus to somewhere close and then a taxi the rest of the way. I had made and paid my own way to the Houston Marathon, and I had made and paid my own way to the London Marathon. I hadn't expected to be doing the same thing for the Olympic Marathon.

When I got to the village, I couldn't get in because I didn't have accreditation. After a few minutes of debate with the security people, I got them to ring the British team, and the Head of Delegation came down to the front gate. Apparently accreditation was at the airport. But I had just come from the airport, and there was no sign of it. Accreditation was at the international airport, but because I had come from Boston, I had been at the domestic airport. Being the Head of Delegation, he had a car, so he drove me to the international airport, and sorted out my security pass.

I was staying in a two bedroom apartment for four. However, there were six of us. Because I was last to arrive, I had the bed in the living room next to the door. All of my room mates were distance runners, and I shared the living area with Tim Hutchings, who ran a brilliant race to finish fourth in the 5,000m.

I had been nervous before I arrived, but once I was in

the village and saw so many fantastic athletes, it hit me hard. I was feeling nervous all day long. I arrived on Monday and by Wednesday I knew I was too wound up. Some of my other room mates, Mike McLeod and Steve Jones, had run the 10,000m and their Olympics were finished. They were going out for a drink that night, so I decided to join them.

I had been meticulous with my diet for weeks, and I had rarely drunk any beer. Going drinking in a bar four days before the race of my life may not sound like the conventional thing to do, but it was an excellent decision. The most important thing for me right then, was to relax and become less nervous. I made two small bottles of beer last all night, and I was back in bed by eleven o'clock. Whilst in the bar, I got talking to a couple of Los Angeles women who didn't believe I was running in the Games. I got the impression that every man they met was using the same line.

I was still nervous the next morning, but it was nowhere near as bad, and I got through the whole day without getting worse. I am sure my night out stopped me from going over the edge. I was running very little in the last couple of days, and with a lot of time to kill, I was always trying to distract myself. There was a cinema in the village and I watched a movie but I couldn't tell you what it was. The Beach Boys played a concert in the village one evening, and I went to see it, but I couldn't tell you any of the songs they played. I had become so focused on the race that my mind couldn't process anything else.

Sunday eventually arrived and the marathon was due to start at 5 o'clock in the afternoon, so I had a full day to get through. I spent a lot of it lying on my bed trying to read a book. I would read for a while, and look at my watch, read for a while and look at my watch. By the early afternoon I was struggling to read at all. After checking the time again, I decided to resist the urge and keep reading. I read and stopped myself looking.

I read some more and stopped myself looking. I resisted several more times and eventually gave in. It was only sixty five seconds since I had last looked. I was so nervous it was distorting my perception of time.

Eventually it was time to go to the bus. I met my team mates, Geoff Smith and Hugh Jones and we sat together for the twenty minute ride to the start. We talked most of the way but I don't know what about. The bus stopped outside the Santa Monica College stadium and as the sun beat down, I walked across the car park and into Chapter 1.

CHAPTER 11

SITTING IN THE ROAD TO SEOUL

My move to the marathon could hardly have gone better. Out of three races I had two wins and an Olympic third. People were saying I should have tried it earlier, because it was obviously my event. I would like to have started earlier and had a longer career over 26 miles, but I moved to the marathon when I was ready to be good at it. For various reasons it took me until I was 31 to develop fully at 10k, and it was the physical and mental qualities I had developed on the track that made me successful when I transferred them to the marathon. I wouldn't have been the same marathon runner without first becoming the best I could be at the shorter distances.

I achieved my targets because I knew what I wanted; I knew why I wanted it; and I knew how much I wanted it. I also stuck to it when things went wrong, and I wasn't distracted by other things that came along. My attitude probably cost me a lot of money along the way. Actually, there is no probably in it, but I wouldn't want to change anything. I never altered my plans to make money, but now that I had an Olympic medal, I had the prospect of making some, and I wasn't going to turn it down. Medallists could expect to be paid by their shoe company for product endorsement, but I already worked for Nike and they didn't want to employ me and sponsor me. We reached a compromise. They continued to pay my salary, while I took a sabbatical year so that I could pursue my running, but with a job to come back to. I went back to Boston, where things had gone so well for me previously.

My old friend, Anne Parker, had moved to a larger house in Auburndale, and there was a spare room to rent, which I happily took. After a few weeks of reasonable training I ran a 10k road race, and came 16th in 30:28. A week later I ran the Freedom Trail road race, put my foot in a pothole after three miles and had to walk back to the finish. After the dizzy heights of Los Angeles, I had fallen back to earth with a severe bump. I didn't really grasp it then, but a curious change was taking place. In the years between LA and the end of my career, I hardly ever ran a decent race, unless it was in a major event.

By successfully peaking for the AAA's 10k and my marathons, I had developed and honed my ability to focus on one event, commit myself to it and then give it everything I had. The more often I pulled this off, the more confident I became that I could do it again. This approach worked for me and it transformed my running career. However, like many things, it had unforeseen consequences. The better I became at digging deep in a major race, the less able I was to run hard in any other event. I tried to do my best, but I became less and less able to produce a performance if a race didn't matter to me.

I had another friend in Boston called John McGrath, who was editor of the magazine, *Boston Running News*. He helped me in a number of ways, and in October '84 he negotiated a $4,000 appearance fee for me to run a 15k road race in Tulsa. I went down to Oklahoma and was treated like a celebrity, until after the race. I finished 16th in 46:33, almost three minutes slower than my best. It was embarrassing. I tried, I never gave up, but I just couldn't perform. The gravy train of appearance fees that an Olympic medallist could expect on the road race circuit, quickly dried up after that, because no one was going to pay good money for such a bad performance.

The week before this I had been to the Windy City to watch the Chicago Marathon. Carlos Lopes and Rob de Castella had both been trounced by Steve Jones, who set a new world best of 2:08:06, in his first attempt at the distance. These were extraordinary times. I had won Houston, won London, and won a bronze at the Olympics, but in the ranking lists produced at the end of the year, I was rated second best marathon runner in Britain.

I continued to train through the winter as usual and expected things to improve. In January I ran the New England indoor 5,000m again. I had achieved a great deal in the four years since my 13:42 epic encounter with Greg Meyer, but it was hard to explain how, as I came last in 14:18. I went down to Florida expecting to turn things round in the Gasparilla 15k, but embarrassed myself again with 33rd in 46:20.

As defending champion, I had arranged to run the London Marathon, and this time I was to be flown over from Boston, given a hotel room for a week and paid a decent appearance fee. This was all good news but I was most concerned about who else was running. I was assured that Steve Jones was not going to compete, and I began my intense period of preparation, thinking about winning. As the race got closer my performances improved, and I started to believe I could run really well again.

Three weeks before the race, I discovered that Steve Jones was running. I didn't care who I ran against, I just wanted to know so I could get my head around it. I always felt that somebody knew he was going to run a long time before I did, but no matter, it was up to me to run the best I could. There were no pacemakers in those days, and Steve and I were in the leading group throughout, as we reached halfway in a decent 64:35. Around the Isle of Dogs the leading group was down to five and the two of us were doing all the leading. I knew we were running a good pace, but I felt alright. Between 19 and 20 miles Jones surged hard and I immediately went with him. Within a few yards the two of us were clear of the rest.

We ran the 21st mile in 4:43, with Jones pushing the pace and me on his shoulder. I felt incredibly alert and alive, but could hardly believe we were going so fast with so far still to run. The marathon course is different now, but back then we ran along the partly paved and partly cobbled streets of Wapping before reaching the Tower of London. We ran 4:48 for each of those two miles. We went past the cheering crowd in front of the Tower hotel, and we hurtled under Tower Bridge side by side. To my amazement, Steve turned to me and asked, 'How do I go to the toilet while I'm running?' (Those weren't the exact words he used, but that was definitely what he meant.) I said, 'You'll have to stop, Steve.'

A hundred yards later, he suddenly disappeared from my peripheral vision. I didn't look round, but I assumed he had taken my advice. I tried to make the most of my advantage, but it was very difficult to accelerate when I was already going so fast. Quarter of a mile later, I glanced behind, and to my horror he was only ten yards back. Moments later he had caught me, and it was clear that whatever he had done with his problem, he was feeling better. As we went through the Blackhall Tunnel he picked up the pace again and I couldn't respond. I maintained a pace of 4:50 per mile all the way to the finish, but he was pulling away from me at about five seconds per mile.

I ran 63:58 for the second half marathon, and about

29:50 for the last 10k, but it just wasn't good enough. My time of 2:08:33 was an English record, which still stands as I write this 24 years later. It would have been a world best if I had run it three years earlier, but standards had leapt forward and it put me eighth on the world all time list. This was another occasion when I was left with mixed emotions. I was delighted to have run so well, but found it hard to understand how I could have run so fast, but still been beaten. I was one of the best marathon runners in the world, but not as good as a Welshman.

There were no major championships in 1985, but both the Commonwealth Games and European championships were due within three weeks of each other in 1986. It was going to be impossible for a marathon runner to do both, and a choice would have to be made. It was still a long way off and I hadn't given it any thought. However, a couple of days after the London race, I was informed that I had been selected to run for England in the Commonwealth Games in Edinburgh. Steve Jones had been picked to run for Britain in the European, and it appeared that Andy Norman, who was still in charge of just about everything, had organised it all. This obviously seemed like a good idea to everybody, because it was assumed that Steve and I could win a championship each. However, it didn't turn out like that. Steve built up a big lead in his race, but then faded badly to plod home in over 2 hours 20 minutes. I was struggling by half way, and I dropped out at 19 miles.

I am not going to try to explain what happened to Jones, because I don't know for sure, but I can tell you what happened to me. I suffered too much from pre-race nerves. I was nervous for months beforehand, and it drained me. I went to the start line with dread instead of anticipation, and I was beaten before the race began. In the past I had always produced my best results in big races with plenty at stake. I had always been nervous, but I had been able to channel that energy into my performance.

So what was different this time? The answer is very simple – it wasn't my goal.

I have mentioned this a few times but I am going to repeat it because it is so important. What do I want? Why do I want it? How much do I want it? Being able to answer these questions to my own satisfaction had always produced my best results. Running the Commonwealth Games 15 months down the line was never my decision. I didn't want it; somebody else wanted it for me. If somebody asked if I would like to be Commonwealth Champion I would say yes, but that's just a conversation; it isn't commitment. The desire to achieve something has to be born inside you, grow inside you and blossom and flourish inside you, until you know what you want, and why you want it, and how much it means. A goal formed this way is an incredibly powerful motivator, but a goal somebody else chooses for you, becomes a burden and then a shackle.

The feeling of nervousness you get before a big race comes from the hormone adrenalin, which is produced in times of fear and stress. Adrenalin raises blood-sugar levels by stimulating glucose production. It increases heart rate and blood flow to the muscles, and it widens the small breathing tubes in the lungs. These are all actions which help you to run faster. Other hormones released by the adrenal gland, like cortisol, are essential for the daily maintenance of systems including blood glucose, blood pressure and the immune response. Like adrenalin, cortisol production is increased by stress, and these 'fight or flight' hormones were essential to us through evolution, as we responded quickly to danger. In days gone by, when you ran away from danger, you could relax as soon as you were safe, and your hormone levels would return to normal. If you are exposed to high levels of cortisol for an extended period of time, it starts to cause lots of problems. It can cause muscle weakness and mental confusion. It decreases fluid retention, and upsets the control of blood sugar levels, and because of our stressful lifestyles, it is believed to be one factor in the diabetes epidemic. These bad effects of cortisol are not what you want when you are trying to run a marathon. I am sure I had far too much cortisol in my system leading up to Edinburgh. I went to the start line in a state of dread, rather than anticipation. I was dehydrated, and I had been unable to add any weight when I did my carbohydrate loading. I was never running well, and when I stopped, I made no clear decision to do so. I just stopped, and wondered what I was doing.

I saw a lot of similarities to this when Paula Radcliffe ran in Athens. She was never going very well, she looked a bit confused when she failed to take the shortest route a couple of times, and when she stopped, it just happened. I was frustrated and annoyed by people who suggested she quit as soon as she couldn't get a medal. I am sure it was cortisol that made her stop, and at the time she didn't know why. Trying to win the Olympics would obviously have been her goal, but she had the enormous stress of knowing that the entire world expected her to win. Coupled with the injury set backs she had before the race, I suspect she was too stressed to perform, as I was in Edinburgh.

Life goes on and a week later I was getting married. I took my running shoes on honeymoon, because I was running the Chicago Marathon eleven weeks later. My training went well, and I went to Chicago six days before the race, hoping to put the dreadful disappointment of Edinburgh behind me. On my first day there I suffered from diarrhoea, and didn't feel well. I felt rough for the next two days, and two days before the race I felt so bad I spent most of the day in bed. I told the organisers about how I was feeling, but that I would wait until race day before making a decision. The race started at 8:45 in the morning, so I didn't have much time to mull it over. I was feeling a little better, so I decided to warm up, and after a mile of jogging I felt alright. I went to the start line telling myself I would be fine, but not feeling convinced.

The opposition included Seko and Salah, and the two of them were in a leading group that was running too fast for my dented confidence. I let them go very early on and ran in the second group. I was feeling alright, and after passing halfway in 64:50, I started to lead my group to maintain the pace. By 16 miles I had only Mike Musyoki for company, and we were catching stragglers from the leading group. With three miles to go I surged away from Musyoki and was quickly catching Salah, but couldn't get to him before the line. Seko won, and I was third in 2:10:13.

There was clearly nothing wrong with me physically. I am sure that all the problems I had suffered before the race were psychosomatic. Th e stress and disappointment of the Commonwealth Games had been so great that my subconscious mind didn't want me to have anything more to do with marathons. After producing a performance in Chicago that made me feel happy and positive, I laid that ghost to rest and I never suffered those problems again.

Throughout the year, I had been having some problems with my left Achilles tendon, and after Chicago it got worse. I had lots of treatment to no avail, and after only managing to average 40 miles a week for three months, I had a cortisone injection from a specialist in Middlesbrough. After this, I was able to train for the 1987 London Marathon, which was the trial for the World Championships. Although it didn't hurt much, there was a small area of skin which was attached to the tendon. I had some very painful friction massage, but the adhesion would not break down.

I went back to the specialist, and asked if he could surgically remove this adhesion. We arranged that I would run

London, and then go in for a quick operation the following weekend. I was hoping to recover quickly from a minor procedure and then train for the World Championships without any niggling pains.

My training wasn't brilliant, but I certainly thought it was good enough to run well. I just needed to produce a big performance. A friend and training partner volunteered to come to the start with me and look after all my kit. I should have said no. The last few minutes before a race begins are the most important, and I had run my greatest races when I had cut myself off from everybody and focused my mind. He was a decent runner but a poor competitor, and although he meant well, he said all the wrong things to me. He filled my mind with all the negativity you could imagine, by saying things like, 'Don't worry; it doesn't hurt until after halfway.' If there is to be any thought at all of the physical pain to come, it should be mentally transferred to your opponents. I should have been saying to myself, 'I am going to give these people hell. I'm going to make them suffer.'

I ran in the leading group for the first six miles, but shortly after the Cutty Shark, Hugh Jones pushed the pace quite hard. With my negative frame of mind, I thought it was too early to be speeding up, and I let him go. I also let nine other runners go with him. I stayed in the second group thinking I would catch the leaders when they slowed. Unfortunately, the lead group didn't slow but my group did, and the gap was getting bigger. Within a mile or two I realised I had made a big mistake, and I picked up my pace. Soon I was running entirely by myself, 150 yards adrift of the leading group, who were bunched together and helping each other. I tried to close the gap, but it was a bit windy and I couldn't get any closer. I became really angry with myself. If only I was on the back of that group. I would be running at the same pace, but it would be so much easier. I would be thinking about winning instead of thinking what a fool I was.

I never managed to catch the leaders. I finished 8th, but only 40 seconds behind the winner. I ran 2:10:32 having run the last 19 miles by myself in a bad mood. Of all the many disappointments I had in my career, this is the only race that still bothers me. I don't know if I could have won the race from the leading group, but I would have tried and I might have done. With one silly mistake induced by a negative attitude, I threw away the chance to be the first man to win London twice.

However, my run was good enough to be picked for the British team for the World Championships in Rome three months later, and if I could quickly clear up my niggling Achilles tendon, perhaps I could produce something much better there. I went in to the Nuffield hospital in Norton as a day patient, because I was only having a local anaesthetic. The anaesthetist tried to produce a nerve block of my whole leg with an injection in my groin, but he must have missed the nerve as nothing happened. The alternative was to inject around the tendon. I tried to lie very still, as I had done ten years earlier.

A few hours after the operation I was allowed to go home, but two days later I had a high temperature and my leg was swelling, because the wound was infected. My GP gave me antibiotics and when I saw the surgeon two days later, he removed the stitches and the blood from a haematoma rushed out. He steri-stripped the sides back together and sent me home. The wound kept oozing blood, and when I went back to see him, he put my ankle in a plaster cast for a week to see if immobilisation would help it to heal. When he took the plaster off, and I saw my leg, I really thought I would never run again.

The skin that had been underneath the stitches had all died and disappeared. There was a hole in my leg about half an inch wide and two inches long, through which you could see the Achilles tendon. He scurried out of the room and came back a few minutes later with a plastic surgeon, who said the only option was to leave it to heal.

The process of healing involves the granulation of new skin from the edges of the wound towards the centre. As time went by, the hole became smaller, but as new skin formed it attached itself to the tendon below. It took about 15 weeks for the wound to heal, and I still have a large wide scar, which is completely attached to the tendon below it. I had gone into hospital to have a small adhesion removed, and now an inch and a half of tendon was completely attached to the skin. Amazingly, it didn't hurt when I ran. Almost four months after London, I was able to jog for ten minutes. I was incredibly unfit, and it took me another two months to work my way back to 65 miles a week.

I was very unhappy about what had happened in that operating theatre. I took legal advice about it, and went to see an independent medical adviser. There were several problems. The presence of anaesthetic at the wound site can interfere with healing. The surgeon had cut out the old scar from my previous operation, which was not what we had agreed, and is not recommended practice. The stitches should have been removed as soon as my leg began to swell, and I shouldn't have become infected in the first place. Having said all that, the expert felt I had been unlucky, and none of it could be regarded as negligent. So, I would just have to get on with it.

After such a long period of enforced rest, I had to increase my training very gradually, because I was getting lots of problems from tight hamstrings to sore knees and stiff calves. I was also having pain in my right Achilles tendon, which was probably caused by the extra stress I had put on that leg while I was on crutches. I was struggling and even simple runs were very tiring.

We were living in an old farm house a few miles north of Newcastle. On a sunny day the quiet country lanes were ideal for running, but at night, in winter, it was a different story. There were no street lights and the only illumination was from the lights of Newcastle reflected from the clouds. I couldn't actually see the road, but I could see where it was because it was a slightly darker shade of grey than the verge, and the hedgerow. I often ran there in total darkness, finding my way mainly from memory. One night after work in December '87, I ran 5 miles along these lanes. I felt bad from the start, and got worse as I ran on. The last mile and a half was all slightly uphill, with a short sharp hill near the house.

I was struggling up the gradient feeling exhausted. I was getting slower and slower. When I reached the bottom of the sharp hill, I stopped. I couldn't face it. I felt so tired I sat down. For about five minutes, I sat in the middle of the cold road, in complete darkness, wondering what I was doing. I had been through so many disappointments in the previous two years, and now I couldn't even run up a little bank. I'd had a great career; perhaps I should pack it all in. The negative voices in my head were becoming persuasive. 'You've been an international athlete, but look at you now. You're 35. Wouldn't you prefer to sit in front of a warm fire on a winter night, instead of sitting in a cold road? You've got nothing more to prove; you've got an Olympic medal.'

It was my negative voices that reminded me that it was almost 1988, and only ten months until the Seoul Olympics. A new voice in my head asked if I wanted to go to the Games again. This would be my last chance; if I didn't go this time there would be no next time. Did I want to go? 'Yes, I did.' Why did I want to go? 'Because it's the greatest competition in the world, and Los Angeles had been the best experience of my life. If I didn't even try to go to the Games I might regret it for the rest of my life.' How much did I want to go? 'I had been through the trauma of dropping out in Edinburgh, and then through the sheer hell of a hole in my leg. I wasn't going to let those things determine the end of my career. The Olympics had defined my career, and I wanted to test myself at the Olympics again.'

I stood up. I knew I was unfit now, but surely I could get fit in ten months. I knew it would be a long, slow process so I started with a compromise. I walked up the hill, and then ran the rest of the way home.

I built up to a decent level of training in the New Year, but it was devoid of any quality. The London Marathon, and Olympic trial, was approaching, and I was short of time. I spoke to Alan Storey, the National marathon coach, and followed his advice by writing to the selectors. I explained that I was over my bad injury, but short of fitness. I would run in the trial to show that I was alright, but I would not be at my best. If they could show the faith to pick me, I was positive I could be at my best by the time of the Games.

I didn't know what sort of performance I needed to produce to sway the selectors, and I went to the start line of the London Marathon with far more hope than expectation. I settled into a large leading group and we passed through halfway in 64:35. I covered the first break after 19 miles, but I couldn't hang on to the second surge at 21. My legs stiffened, and I felt dreadful as I plodded to the finish. I came 10th in a personal worst of 2:12:28. There were five Britons in front of me; Kevin Forster, Hugh Jones, Dave Long, Allister Hutton and John Wheway. I had produced a good performance, considering my preparation, but I didn't expect to be picked in front of so many others. If I hadn't written that letter I don't think I would have been considered, but it did the trick and I was named in the team with Kevin and Hugh.

A month after London my first child, Joe, was born.

My diary records no more than four sleepless nights, so I can't blame him for the poor training I was doing. I was cutting a lot of my sessions short because of niggles, or simply because I was struggling to do them. Physiotherapy wasn't making me any better, so I went down to London for some biomechanical testing. It appeared that I was too inflexible in my hips and especially my calf muscles, and it was this muscular tightness that was causing my problems. I did regular stretching exercises but they weren't enough, and I had to do more.

Ten weeks before the Games I ran the Great North Run Half Marathon. I finished 11th in 64:31. The race was won by John Treacy in 61:00. He had beaten me by two seconds in the Olympic marathon four years earlier, but now, as we both prepared for Seoul, he was beating me by three and a half minutes over half the distance. This was a bad situation and I knew I had to come up with a positive angle on it. So I applied considerable mental dexterity to the normal rules of logic, and decided this result clearly showed I would beat Treacy in Seoul. I figured that for him to run so well, he must have peaked already, whereas I was going to peak in ten weeks time. I told myself that by the Games he could only get worse, and I could only get better. If he had beaten me by only a minute I would have been worried about him!

Seoul, just like every Olympic marathon, was going to be ridiculously hot, and we would all have to acclimatise. The British Team were having a pre-Games training camp in the comparable heat of Japan, but I had heard that it was a very poor venue for long distance running. I preferred the idea of going back to Boston, where I knew I could train properly. My club mate and team mate, Kevin Forster, wanted to come too. I asked my old friend, John McGrath, if he knew anybody who needed some house-sitters during the summer. He went further than that. He put an advert in his magazine offering one lucky reader the chance to host two Olympic runners.

I got a phone call one afternoon in my office at Nike, from Steve Kahian of Lakeville, Massachusetts, who had seen the advert. He had a three bedroom house, which we could have, while he moved into the guest apartment above his garage. There was plenty of space so we could bring our families, and he had two spare cars so we could drive one each. Kevin and I were there for four weeks with our wives and children, and Steve let us live as if the house belonged to us. Wherever I have been in the world, I have always found that if you are genuinely and honestly trying to do your best at something, people seem to appear out of nowhere to help you. Steve was very generous to us and I think he enjoyed telling his friends that two marathon runners were using his house for Olympic preparation.

I managed some decent training in the heat and humidity of August in New England, including 5 x one mile in 4:38 with a lap recovery in 90 seconds; 5 x 1000m in 2:48 with 30 seconds recovery; a 28 mile run and a 20 mile interval run with surges of 1, 2 or 4 minutes duration every 5 minutes. It was nearly ten months since I had committed myself to Seoul whilst sitting in the road in the December darkness, and some of my sessions were making me believe I might not embarrass myself when I got there. My race results, however, were embarrassing. Kevin and I raced twice on this trip and he trounced me at the Falmouth road race, where I finished 30th in 34:24, which was 77 seconds slower than my time 7 years earlier. He then beat me out of sight, in our last race before the Games, at the New Haven 20k where I ran 63 minutes, which is equivalent to a half marathon in about 66:30. It was a very humid day, but two months prior to this I had reconciled my disappointment at running 64:30 in the Great North Run with an assurance that, as the Games got closer, I was going to get better and better. Clearly something wasn't working.

The training and heat acclimatisation had gone well enough, and Steve's place was a lot more comfortable than a training camp in Japan, but we now faced a lot of travelling. We flew back across the Atlantic and up to Newcastle, and four days later Kevin and I were flying back to London and on to Seoul via Anchorage and Tokyo. We arrived at the Olympic village, very jet-lagged and tired, eleven days before the marathon. We had to give ourselves that much time to make sure we were fully adjusted to the time change, but it is a long time to spend in an Olympic village waiting for your race. As usual, the marathon was the last event, and as the days went by the atmosphere around the village changed as more people finished their competitions.

A lot of athletes spent their time in the city, especially at some of the markets, where expensive designer goods were available at huge discounts. Apparently, I missed out on some fantastic bargains, because I never ventured out of the village except for training runs. I spent most of that week and a half lying on my bed doing crossword puzzles. I found that a crossword required enough concentration to be distracting, but allowed me to flip in and out of it much more easily than the concentration needed to read a novel. I finished an entire book of puzzles while other people were shopping, because I reckoned that walking the hot streets in search of a cheap watch was going to use up some of my energy. I knew that come race day, I was going to need every single scrap of physical and mental energy that I could muster. I wanted to save all of it.

The race was scheduled for 2:30 in the afternoon because that's when American television wanted it; despite the fact that it was hot and the sun was so bright. If you wanted to stage a mass participation marathon in the conditions that nearly always face Olympic marathon runners, you wouldn't get permission to do it, because it would be regarded as unsafe. However, I gave no thought to the weather as I rode on the

162

bus to the stadium. I was too busy battling my thoughts. I had gone to Los Angeles believing I would run the race of my life, and feeling very nervous because I didn't know what that would bring me and what my limit was. I had been full of excited anticipation. But now, as I travelled to the start in Seoul, I was very nervous again but what I felt was closer to dread. I hadn't run a good race for two years; I knew my training was barely adequate, and I felt a lot of pressure to perform because the selectors had picked me instead of the people who had beaten me in the trial. If there was a limit for me to consider, it was to do with how badly I might run, not how well.

Four years earlier I had controlled my pre-race mental turmoil by telling myself that what I faced was not a problem but a fantastic opportunity. I had been a 33/1 outsider, who was in great shape, with everything to gain and nothing to lose. This time I couldn't use the same approach because I was a previous medallist who wasn't in great shape. What I faced was the opportunity to embarrass myself and have everybody say that I shouldn't have been picked ahead of others, just on my past performance.

As I sat in the shade watching some of my competitors doing far more laps of the warm-up track than I thought necessary in this heat, I made myself get a grip. I rejected all thoughts of what other people may or may not think. I rejected all elaborate and complicated thoughts. I concentrated on simple, obvious things that were going to help me. I concentrated on this simple mental sequence: where are you, Charlie? 'I am about to run the Olympic marathon.' What have you wanted to do all your life? 'Run in the Olympics.' How come you think you have a problem?

I thought about all the injuries and setbacks I had been through, and realised that despite them all I was here, and I was about to compete in the greatest race in the world. I told myself that I was supposed to be here, and because it was the Olympic Games I would produce a performance worthy of the occasion. I realised this really was an opportunity. It was an opportunity to show myself what I was made of.

The early pace was faster than most people were expecting in such hot conditions. After quarter of an hour of running I had a brief conversation. I don't know if it was just coincidence or whether he felt the need to continue the interchange we had started four years earlier in Los Angeles, but it was Rob de Castella who spoke to me. He saw me check my watch at 5,000 metres and he asked what pace we were on. I told him we were doing about 2:09 pace, to which he replied, 'In this heat – we are all going to die!' As a reply I simply shrugged my shoulders, but I was thinking, 'That's a very negative thing for him to say. Perhaps my friend from last year's London marathon got to him before the start. I think I can beat him today if that's how he is thinking.' I then smiled to myself when I realised I clearly had my racing head on. We were only three miles into the race, and I was telling myself I had de Castella beaten!

Despite the heat and the decent early pace, there was a very large group at the front. I was content to be one of the 33 runners in the leading pack after 15 kilometres, but the size of the group was causing huge problems at the drink stations. It was very hard to see and then grab my drink with so many people in the way, and I missed two out of the first three. The problem was made much worse than it should have been by the organisers. They insisted that everyone could have their own drink at each station, but there would be no other drinks available.

In Los Angeles, the race had been organised by people who understood the marathon, and who knew how bad the heat was for running. They had provided tables for individual drinks, but if you missed your own drink, there were tables with water a hundred yards later. They also organised showers across the road, with a fine mist of water you could run through. There was none of that in Seoul. This marathon had been organised by people with a rule book, and they were going to stick exactly to the rules. They completely failed to appreciate that when the rule book on marathon drink stations had been written, nobody had contemplated holding a major championship race in these conditions. I got the British team manager to ask for a water table beyond the individual drinks, and I know that other countries asked for it too, but the Koreans were determined to stick exactly to the rules as laid down in their book, and our request was denied.

We ran on under the hot sun. The group was down to 24 as we passed 20 kilometres in 61:21. We went through the half marathon in about 64:50, and as we crossed the Han-Gang River, I found myself at the front. I led for a few hundred yards and enjoyed the feeling of leading. It made me really confident that I was performing well, but I didn't want to stay there so I dropped in behind Juma Ikangaa, who still loved to take the pace.

By 25 kilometres the group was down to 13, and I was still there. Doing well in the Olympic marathon is really simple. Get yourself in the leading group and just stay there while everybody else drops off. Like most things in life, it's simple, but not easy! I was still there but I wasn't finding it easy.

With about 20 miles behind us I knew the real action would be happening soon. I was very hot and tired, but I was making myself very focused. We approached a drinks station and I moved forward to get a clear sight of my bottle. I had to get a drink. I concentrated intently. I saw it, grabbed it and lifted it off the table without a break in stride. I raised it to my mouth and drank. I spluttered and gagged. It must have been standing in direct sunshine all day because it was hot. It was the temperature of a freshly made coffee. I suppose hot water is still water but it was the shock of putting something so warm in my mouth that affected me. The surprise gave me an adrenalin spurt, which knocked my equilibrium. Then the adrenalin wore off and I had the downshift that follows. Half a mile later I was struggling. I felt flat and empty. Gelindo Bordin, Juma Ikangaa, Ahmed Salah, Douglas Wakihuri and Takeyuki Nakayama were all moving away from me. I was isolated in 6th and the leading group was getting further away with every stride.

'No! No! No!' I had to talk myself through this. I had to badger myself through this. 'You can't get dropped now. Six miles is too far to run alone. They'll catch you from behind. You have to get a grip. Come on. Concentrate. Focus. It's just a bad spell. You can get through it. Posture! You're slumping. Straighten up. Shoulders back, chin down, look up. Come on. You're not going to fade away. Come on. Hold that gap. You must not fade. This is the Olympics.' Those last four words helped to change me from panic to commitment. 'This is the Olympics. I have to close that gap. I have to catch them. Come on. I have to catch them. I have to do an effort. A four minute effort from my interval run. Start now. Go. Pick it up. Come on. That's it. Quicken. Yes. Focus. Stay smooth. I'm holding them. I can do this. I have to do this. I will do this. Come on. It's closing. Fifty yards. Focus on them. Long strides. Loose hands. More effort. That's it. Hold this. Come on. Come on. It's working. Forty yards. I wish they would slow down. How fast are they going if I can't catch them running this hard? Concentrate. Focus. I am catching them. Hold this effort. Hold it. Hold it. Come on. That's the Olympic marathon leading group thirty yards away, and I am catching them. Hold this speed. No faster. It takes time to close a gap. It takes as long as it takes. Come on. Come on. Come on. I'm catching them. It's working. Twenty yards. Don't surge to close it. Hold this effort. Hold it. Hold it. Concentrate.

Focus. Concentrate. Focus. It's working. Ten yards. Come on. I am going to do it. Come on. Five yards. Stay smooth. Long strides. Nearly there. Come on. Come on. Come on. Done it. Yes. Leading group of six, and I'm in it. Relax. Relax. Relax.'

As I reached the back of the group, two of them looked round in surprise. As they wondered where I had come from, I prayed to a god I don't believe in. I prayed that nobody was going to pick up the pace for at least a couple of miles, because I was going to need a long spell of even paced running to recover from that effort. In my 20 mile interval training session, I ran for five minutes at six minutes per mile between my efforts. But that's training, and here in the race I was trying to recover at five minutes per mile.

We ran together for less than a mile before another surge came, and everybody went with it, except me. I wanted to go with it, and I tried to go with it, but nothing happened. I put in more effort, but I didn't move any faster. They were moving away from me again, but I couldn't do anything about it. I was empty. I knew I wasn't going to be able to produce any more efforts because to keep going for the last four miles was going to take a long, hard continuous effort. I had to concentrate and focus. I had to hold myself together.

The leaders were moving away with every stride, but after a few minutes Ikangaa was dropped from the group. He was a long way ahead, but I fixed my mind and my gaze onto him. I had raced him twice before and beaten him each time. I was incredibly tired and my legs felt dead, but he gave me something to aim at. Trying to catch him stopped me thinking about how far it still was to the finish. The gap between us slowly closed, and eventually I got past him. I was hurting, but I was fifth. I had always thought that if I couldn't get a medal I would try to be fourth. If I couldn't be fourth I would try to be fifth. Fifth wasn't bad.

As I ran on I knew Ikangaa was beaten, but the others were out of sight in front of me. This part of the course was tree-lined and there were no spectators, and no officials. It was very strange. I was fifth in the Olympic marathon, running as hard as I could along an empty, silent road, all by myself. Unfortunately, my isolation didn't last as long as I had hoped. I heard footsteps behind me. I didn't look round – I knew what was happening. The footsteps got closer, and it was the Australian, Steve Moneghetti, who came past me. I would normally try to latch on to somebody as they went past, but I didn't try to because I knew that any change in my cadence or rhythm was likely to tip me over the edge that I was clinging to.

If I can't be fourth, I'll be fifth. If I can't be fifth, I'll be sixth. If I can't be sixth….no, no, no. I will not be seventh. I must hang on to sixth. Sixth is alright. Seventh is nowhere. I have to hold on to this.

I turned a corner, which I knew was two miles from the finish. It was a straight wide road, disappearing into the distance. It also meant turning directly towards the sun. It was getting lower in the sky, but I still felt its heat against my face and arms. I was hot, tired and dehydrated. I was struggling.

Your leg muscles contract to propel you forward, and to absorb the pounding of the road, but they also have to stretch to take your legs through the extensive movement of a runner's gait. The elasticity in your muscles decreases with age, lack of training, and excessive pounding on a hard surface. My leg muscles were getting tighter, and tighter and tighter. Four years earlier, as I ran towards the Coliseum, I was tired and hurting, but I was moving smoothly, and as I flowed along the road I felt as if I had wheels beneath my torso. But here in Seoul, as every footstep jarred through my body, I felt as if I was running on wooden stumps.

I was still trying to tell myself that sixth is ok and

168

seventh is nowhere, but my body was screaming at me to slow down. All the little voices in my head were saying stop, sit down, lie down, you'll feel better. I was in trouble. I was in big trouble and I still had a mile and three quarters to run. I had to think of something drastic, and something drastic came to mind. I made a deal. I made a pact with myself. If I could keep this going to the finish line I would never have to run another marathon. To get through this, I needed all the thoughts in my head to work together. A promise was made and we agreed. After all the running we had done, we could manage one more mile and a half, no matter how hard it was.

I was running on empty, and I couldn't ignore the pain in my legs, but I shut out every other thought, and focused on running. I forgot about the stadium, and I forgot about the finish line, and I narrowed my thoughts down and down to a single point – running. The finish line would come eventually, but for now I had to run a yard, and then another one.

I held on for sixth and finished in 2 hours 12:19. Gelindo Bordin won it in 2:10:32, with Wakihuri second, and Salah took the bronze a minute and twenty seconds ahead of me. Nakayama was fourth and Moneghetti beat me by 30 seconds. Behind me, there was a bigger gap than I had imagined. Ikangaa was 47 seconds back, with de Castella a second behind him. Toshihiko Seko was ninth.

Lindsay and I have looked at my '88 training diary several times, and there is nothing in it to suggest I was going to run the way I did. There is a conclusion to be drawn from this. If you don't believe the mind is the most important factor in athletic performance, it's quite simple – you are wrong. The chance to run this race wasn't handed to me out of the blue like the Commonwealth Games; it was a goal I had made sitting on a cold, dark road when I was too tired to run up a hill. If you don't believe it is vital to know what you want, why you want it and how much you want it, it's quite simple – you are wrong.

After the race they took the entire first ten for a drug test. We all had to sit around in a very small room waiting to pee. Everybody was so dehydrated we were there for what seemed like hours. With the help of some beer, that I really didn't feel like having, I managed to do what I had to do. As I left the room I was met by Simon Turnbull, who was the Athletics writer for the Newcastle Journal. His first question was, 'I know you are 36 now, but surely you aren't going to retire after a performance like that?'

CHAPTER 12

PROGRESS OF TRAINING

My father used to be interested in horse racing, and he was a friend of one of the most successful trainers in the North East. When I met him, I took the opportunity to talk about his training methods. I was shocked at how little his horses did compared to runners. Th e regime he and other trainers used sounded very old fashioned to me, so I did some research, and wrote an article comparing the development of athletic performance with that of horse racing. I compared the world record for the mile with the winning time in the Derby. I thought that was fair because the Derby has been run over the same course for well over a century and always attracted the very best horses.

Walter George broke the world record for the mile in 1886, when he ran 4 minutes 12.75 seconds. In 1999 the record was reduced to 3:43:13 by Hicham El Guerrouj. Th at is an improvement of about 29 seconds, which is 12%. The winner of the Derby in 1910 ran it in 2 minutes 35 seconds. The winner in 2008 took 2:36, and the fastest time in recent years is 2:32. With the exception of a few years where the race has been run slowly, the Derby is always won between 2:32 and 2:36. In other words, there has been no improvement at all in the last hundred years.

In my article, I suggested this difference might be down to training methods. If it was possible to train a horse to show the same improvement as humans had done, you could win the Derby by over 200 yards; or you could take a horse that was simply decent, and turn it into a Derby winner.

I was very naïve at the time because I sent this article off to a horse-racing magazine that my dad used to read, simply hoping to be published. Of course, it was never published because whoever opened the envelope would have realised that if what I was saying was true, it would be worth millions of pounds to the trainer who could achieve it. I heard nothing more about the article, but a little while later some of the best-known running coaches started getting phone calls from Newmarket's finest racing yards.

It is over thirty years since I wrote that article, and the winning time for the Derby still hasn't changed at all. The reason is probably that horses in the Derby are all three year olds, and they don't have time to go through the long process of development that runners use. I should have concentrated on winners of the Grand National, which are typically nine or ten years old. Perhaps horses just cannot be developed in the same way as humans, who continue to run faster thanks to ever-improving training methods. This human progress at middle distance running can be traced to the ideas of a small number of pioneering coaches.

The work of Harry Andrews is not well known, but it is interesting. His book *Training for Athletics, and Health* was first published in 1903; my copy is the fourth edition which appeared in 1911, suggesting this was a popular book at the time.

Harry Andrews was clearly a successful coach. His

methods produced athletes whose performances live forever in the annals of athletics' history. Who could forget such famous names as Frank Shoreland, Blatt Betts and Montague Holbein? No, I haven't heard of them either, but I have heard a lot about his star pupil, Alfred Shrub, who set world records at every distance from one and a half miles to the hour run.

Alf and the boys used to do all their training on the track. It was regarded as inappropriate to run through the streets in 1903, and of course, this was 70 years pre-Nike so the footwear wasn't suitable for too much road running. Walking was the basis of the Andrews' training system; lots of brisk walking, at least four to six miles per day, before breakfast, before lunch, before supper and before retiring. Running was reserved for two or three occasions per week, and was always related to the racing distance.

A typical schedule for any distance up to six miles would be:
For two weeks, three times a week:

1 mile further than race distance at ¾ speed.
For the next two weeks, three times a week:

½ race distance at your best speed
On one day in this period:

Race distance trial at your best effort. (I wonder how many world records Alfred Shrub set that didn't count, because he did them in training.)

Extremely long races were popular at the time, and for everything over 15 miles, he suggested 7 or 8 miles, three times per week. Certain stimulants were in common use at the time, but Andrews felt that the use of strychnine was overrated, and cocaine lozenges were definitely not a good idea! He did recommend some substances in the closing stages of very long races. His favourite was half a sponge cake soaked in champagne, 25 minutes before the end. This could be followed 10 minutes later with a third of a tumbler of wine to ensure a strong finish.

He clearly didn't expect his athletes to be teetotal, but smoking was not allowed, and being the correct weight was vital. The most gifted athlete he ever saw was W. G. George, whose world mile record, which I mentioned earlier, was a performance that he thought would probably never be beaten.

His book contains advice for everyone, and he says, 'I believe that there are very few people who would not derive benefit from a moderate course of training. A walk before breakfast is in my opinion worth all the medicine in the world. To the average individual it will be a hard and gruelling task for the first fortnight; but let him take heart from this very fatigue, for it is the surest proof that he is in need of what he is doing.' So, here is a man, from over a century ago, with advice that if heeded would probably have prevented the epidemics of obesity, heart disease and diabetes that now afflict us.

Dr Woldemar Gerschler made his mark on the sport about thirty years after Andrews. Gerschler was a professor of physical education in Freiburg, Germany. In contrast to Andrews' steady running around the track, he developed a method of running short distances at high intensity, repeated often, with short breaks and incomplete recovery. In other words, he invented interval training. His methods were first made famous by Rudolf Harbig who, in 1939, set a world record for 800m of 1:46.6, which stood for 16 years.

In interval training, speeds are constantly practised that are faster than the runner's race pace. This speed training increases the ability of the body to run with an oxygen debt, and the runner learns to run hard in a state of fatigue. The runs are over 100 and 200 meters, with occasional use of 400 meters, and the efforts have to be intense. The number of times the runs are repeated depends upon the fitness of the runner, but at least 10 and up to 40 repetitions could be used in a session.

The interval between each effort was the important

thing. Gerschler worked with cardiologist, Herbert Reindel, to establish the Gerschler-Reindel Law to determine the length of an interval. 'The running effort in interval training should send the heart rate to around 180 beats per minute. From this point, the heart is allowed 90 seconds to return to 120-125 beats per minute. If the latter takes longer, the effort has been either too violent or too long. When the pulse returns to 120-125 beats per minute, the runner should begin running again, even if it takes less than 90 seconds to recover.'

Apparently, there are people who enjoy a bit of Germanic regimentation, coupled with physical pain, but going to the track everyday to run fast repetitions until you can't do it any more doesn't sound like a lot of fun to me.

In 1947 another German, Dr Ernst van Aaken, published his pure-endurance training method for long distance runners. It is completely different to interval training, but just as one-dimensional.

Van Aaken believed that man has the speed but not the endurance to run well, and that two to six years of endurance training, good physical condition and light body weight are essentials. Light body weight was one of his obsessions. He coached Harold Norpoth, who was the most emaciated man ever to win an Olympic medal. He recommended athletes to eat small quantities of highly nutritious foods. That sounds fair enough – but how small? For six days a week very small, and on the seventh, you were to eat nothing at all. Of course, alcohol was out, and you were advised not even to look at a cream cake.

Van Aaken believed that since oxygen was needed for a fire to burn, it was also needed to burn off fat. He also believed that athletes should never dip into their reserves, except when racing, and therefore, if you ran without getting breathless, your heart was pumping lots of oxygen-rich blood around your body, burning calories and increasing your endurance, all without making you too tired. He recommended daily doses of this, depending upon your condition, of between six and fifty miles!

Mihaly Igloi produced a group of world record breaking Hungarians in the 1950s, and then moved to America and repeated his feat in the early 60s. However, he had little success after that.

Like Gerschler, he had his athletes on the track every day, but he used repetitions instead of intervals. The difference is that he believed the distance run was more important than the rest in between, and so, for his athletes to maintain their pace over a repeated distance, they could take longer rests as they tired. He didn't write training schedules because all his training was on a personal basis.

Igloi, like Gerschler and van Aaken, had some success because there is some validity in their methods, but their results have been left far behind, because they are so one-dimensional.

The man to solve that problem was Arthur Lydiard of New Zealand. He was the first coach to introduce a long-range training plan with distinct periods of different training. It was all designed to bring an athlete to peak performance for the most important race of the year. It worked extremely well, as a number of his athletes proved with their collection of Olympic medals in the 1960s. Lydiard was a decent runner, and he developed his system after experimenting on himself, and then on other runners.

There are three phases to his method:

Marathon Training - Whether you are training for the marathon or the mile, you need as much endurance as possible, and this you get from running as many miles as your ability will allow. He recommends a variety of terrain and pace during this phase, but it must include lots of long runs.

Hill Training - This phase lasts six weeks. The idea is to add specific leg and ankle strength to your highly developed basic conditioning. The ideal hill is both steep and long, and you are supposed to bound up it with an exaggerated knee lift and extensive push from the ankles. This is done three times a week, and on alternate days you work on leg speed. Lots of short sprints, especially on a slight downhill gradient, will reduce the 'viscosity of the muscles' and prepare you for the work required in the third phase. On the seventh day you do a long easy run to maintain the endurance you built up in phase one.

Speed Training - This is another six-week period that develops speed and puts the final racing edge to all the work you have already done. It consists of a steadily increasing, and balanced intensity of track repetitions, which teach you to run faster and cope with fatigue.

These were all the options when I joined the sport, and a runner, or his coach, had a lot of decisions to make. He had to decide how many miles to run; how many hills to do; how many intervals and repetitions to run; what speed to run; what rest to take; and how much sponge cake soaked in champagne to consume. When I started training it was only five years after Lydiard's most famous athlete, Peter Snell, had won the 800 metre/1500 metre double at the 1964 Tokyo Olympics, and most people were adopting his methods.

I followed Lydiard's basic methods for years, but with only limited success. Throughout all those years, when I was running alright but not fulfilling myself, I was doing a winter of steady running to build endurance, and then having two problems when I tried to sharpen for track races. I often suffered injury when I started running faster, and it would take me a long time and several track races to get any quicker.

I think Lydiard's method worked wonderfully for someone like Snell, who was naturally very fast, and just needed to add endurance to his speed, but someone devoid of real speed, like me, needed to maintain some faster running all the time.

I discovered the importance of this during my year in Boston, when after doing a few indoor track sessions, I ran 13:42 for 5,000 metres in January, and went on to have a good summer. Some faster running throughout the year did two things for me: firstly, it kept my muscles attuned to the extra stress of faster running, resulting in less stiffness and fewer injuries; secondly, it improved my lactic acid tolerance.

Lactic acid is a by-product of muscular energy production without sufficient oxygen. It causes the stinging pain in the muscles when you run fast for too long, and it is a major limiting factor in middle to long distance running performance. Without fully realising it at the time, I was training my bio-chemical systems to deal with lactic acid when I was doing my winter track sessions at my 5,000 metre race pace.

For years I, and most other runners, had a simplistic approach: run a lot of miles to develop endurance, and then run fast to develop speed; put the two together and race well. When training like this, I ran dozens of track races where I was going well, but would fade badly over the last two or three laps. I always thought I needed to do more speed work to make me faster, but I was wrong. I didn't need speed I needed lactic acid tolerance. We all used to run slowly for stamina, and quickly for speed, and think we were ready to race, but we rarely trained at race pace.

Training at race pace develops the specific bio-chemical systems and enzymes that deal with lactic acid at that intensity. Your body is badly equipped to do that, if a race is the first time you run at that pace. Lactate tolerance training is one of two developments that have taken performances on to new levels. The other is aerobic threshold running, which I mention later. Lactate tolerance works by running repetitions on the track at your race pace, and increasing these sessions, so that you can run further and further into your race distance without suffering from oxygen debt. These sessions can be carefully controlled by taking fingertip blood tests in between the efforts and measuring the levels of lactate in the blood. There are hand held machines available that can produce a reading in 45 seconds, from just one drop of blood.

A certain amount of lactate is produced at low levels of exercise, and the concentration at which it usually starts to become a problem is 4 millimoles (mmols) per litre of blood. A well-trained runner can often run 5,000m at 7, 8 or 9 mmols, and the great athletes, who can sprint the last lap of such a race, can push the level up to anything from 14 to 20 mmols.

By training at race pace, you can develop the ability to run with high concentrations of blood lactate, and maintain your pace. During a track session at race pace the level of blood lactate should be almost constant, and increase only slightly. If it goes up rapidly, the session is too hard. If it doesn't increase at all, it is too easy. When you can perform a session at almost constant lactate levels, you are ready to add the final stage of race preparation, which consists of tolerance to extreme levels of lactate, which you need for the last lap. This is achieved by very fast running with very short recovery. It needs to be the final stage of training, because it will quickly make you over-trained and over the top if you don't have the race pace lactate tolerance that comes before it. And, of course, you also have to have a lot of aerobic endurance too.

I used to do some runs that involved a sustained effort at high intensity, because it felt the right thing to do. This type of training has developed considerably since my day, thanks to advances in technology.

The aerobic threshold run has become a vital component in the development of runners. It involves running for 20 to 25 minutes at a speed that is right on the edge of your aerobic ability. In other words, you don't get out of breath, but any faster and you would. These sessions push back the threshold, and allow you to run further and faster, before you get into oxygen debt and start to produce too much lactic acid. The effort required is related to your heart rate, and after determining your heart rate at the threshold, you can perform these runs with the help of a heart rate monitor. Lindsay Dunn pioneered the use of heart rate monitors in relation to these sessions, and developed a method to gauge an athlete's threshold, without the need for laboratory tests.

A heart rate monitor consists of a thin elasticated strap around the chest, containing a sensor that transmits the heart rate to a digital display on the runner's wrist. While wearing this device, Lindsay has his runners perform a 20 to 25 minute run at their half marathon race pace. After eight minutes of running, when bodily systems should be stabilised, the runner checks their pace over a measured distance, and then checks it again after about nineteen minutes of running. The two measured sections are to ensure the run is performed at a constant pace, and at the correct pace. If the pace is constant, the heart rate should increase by a few beats per minute as the athlete becomes more tired. Typically, a runner will record 160 beats per minute during this run. In the latter stages it should go up to about 163. If this happens, a runner can confidently accept their aerobic threshold is reached at 160 beats per minute. If the heart rate doesn't increase at all. the effort is too low, and if it goes up too much, the effort is too hard. Lindsay reckons it only ever takes two or three attempts to establish an accurate threshold level.

He credits these threshold runs with a great deal of the improvement in many of his athletes. When they handle these sessions well, he introduces a variation in which the session starts at 5 beats per minute below threshold, then increases to threshold pace, and finishes at 5 beats above threshold pace. He can be mean like that!

The conventional wisdom on altitude training is well known. At altitudes higher than 2,000 metres above sea level there is less air pressure, and therefore less oxygen. When you live and train there, your body compensates for the lack of oxygen by increasing the production of red blood cells. This acclimatisation takes about three weeks. When you return to sea level, the extra red cells have increased your oxygen carrying capacity, and, therefore, your performance should improve.

The disadvantages of high altitude running are caused by the lack of oxygen. It is impossible to train at the same intensity and speed that you would have done at sea level. This has led some athletes to spend extended periods of time at altitude, running everything quite slowly. I do not understand how training to run slowly makes you a better runner, despite achieving the holy grail of an increased haematocrit. (Haematocrit is a measure of red blood cell concentration.)

Lindsay Dunn has a different approach to all of this and I agree with him. Lindsay has taken several groups of athletes to altitude and invariably had success. His approach is to reduce the distances but run quickly in both the steady runs and track sessions. Neither can be done as quickly they would be at sea level, but a fast pace, with reduced oxygen, produces a considerable training effect upon the entire cardio vascular system, from the pumping heart to the chemical processes at cellular level. When you return to sea level you can train the muscular and nervous systems to run faster because the cardiovascular system is no longer such a limiting factor. To achieve this progress at sea level requires such hard training that it risks injury.

Most coaches will say that it is pointless going to altitude for less than three weeks. If all you want to do is maximise red blood cells they are right, but with Lindsay Dunn's approach, you can gain benefits in as few as ten days.

All the progress I have mentioned has come from

challenging the conventional wisdom of the time, and learning from what others are doing. In a constant search for improvement, good coaches will look beyond their own ideas and learn from the methods of successful athletes. I was always a little surprised that nobody asked me how I prepared for the Olympic marathon in the heat of Los Angeles. (Nobody asked me, apart from Lindsay who took a photocopy of my entire 1984 training diary.) I don't pretend to have all the answers, and I don't know if other runners were already doing the same thing, but one of the most important sessions I did was a 15 mile run at three quarter effort. I felt that I had to get used to maintaining a brisk pace over an extended distance, and I ran intuitively at a pace that was brisk, but sustainable, for 15 miles. To run like that for 20 miles would be too hard, and to run for 10 miles would lack relevance for the marathon. I always thought this session was an important part of my training.

Several years later, a group of Italian scientists and coaches produced an article in which they claimed that the regular use of a 90 minute run at a blood lactate level of 3 mmols was a primary reason for the success of Italian marathon runners. (They have produced two Olympic champions, in 1988 and 2004.) If you remember from earlier, 4 mmols of lactate is generally the aerobic threshold, so this run should be performed at three quarters of that effort, which is precisely what I had been doing.

My point in highlighting this is not to make myself look clever: the point is that I was doing something that was later proved by science to be the right thing to do, and there must be other people having success because they are doing something that is just right for their event. The sharing of knowledge and innovation pushes forward the performance of athletes. If your coach thinks he knows everything, my advice is simple - get another coach.

I had problems with my Achilles tendons throughout my career, and I have already gone through some of the gory details of the surgery I underwent. I spent a great deal of time, and quite a bit of money, lying on treatment tables with ultra sound and infra red equipment applied to my tendonitis, without very much success. I was treated using the conventional wisdom of the time, but nowadays there is a new approach that I am certain would have helped me to avoid the problems and surgery I endured.

Specialists in sports injuries now appreciate that pain in one location is often caused by a problem somewhere else. My tendons were sore, so my tendons were treated, but it didn't work well because the real problems were tightness and scar tissue in my calf muscles. The reduced mobility in my calves transferred the stress to my tendons, making them sore. Modern treatment would involve massage deep into the muscle to break down the tightness and scar tissue, which would relieve the pressure on the tendon.

I had weekly deep massage when I was in America and avoided serious injury. If I had been able to have it throughout my career, I would have had far fewer interruptions to my training, and I could have been a better runner.

My career improved enormously when I developed a new mental approach. I had no expertise in sports psychology; I just cobbled my ideas together from things I had read, how I felt and what seemed to work. When I got it right, it worked extremely well, but I didn't always get it right. If I'd had a sports psychologist working with me before the Commonwealth Games and the 1987 London marathon, I am positive I would have done much better in those events. Nobody had sports psychologists in those days, but they do now. British Cycling regards their psychologist as an essential member of the team.

Athletics needs to follow their lead.

If I, or any of my contemporaries, were running now we would have fewer serious injuries thanks to the progress in treatment. We would be able to train more scientifically, thanks to the developments in training, technology and psychology. We would have less pressure to earn a living, thanks to the money that is available through lottery funding. With all these benefits I believe that most, if not all, the British runners I competed against would have produced faster times if they were running now, than they did in the 1980s.

So why, why, why, are today's best British runners running slower times than we did twenty to thirty years ago?

CHAPTER 13

WHAT HOPE OLYMPIC MEDALS ?

Britain will be hoping for success in as many sports as possible when the Olympic Games come to London in 2012. I am sure those hopes will be realised in certain sports like cycling, but I fear that in athletics we will struggle. I hope I am proved wrong, but I expect disappointment on the track in general and failure amongst male distance runners in particular.

The success of Paula Radcliffe and Mo Farah, over recent years, has deflected some of the attention away from a drastic decline in standards. The success of one or two people is not the way to judge the health of a sport, so I have looked at the all-time top 100 British runners in the distance events, and compared decades. I realise as I write this in 2009 that this decade has another year to go, but even allowing for that, the figures are startling.

I compared the number of men in the top 100 who ran their performance in this decade, with the number who are in the top 100 from the 1980s. Over 5,000m there are 13 from this decade and 43 from the eighties. Over 10,000m it is 9 from the noughties and 34 from the eighties, and at the marathon the figures are 7 from now and 50 from then.

I didn't think it was fair to compare the women's lists in the same way, because these three events only became available to women during the eighties. However, despite the first women's Olympic marathon being in 1984, the British list has 35 entries from the eighties compared to 25 from this decade.

The world level has moved forward a long way in thirty years. Ninety of the top 100 performances for the men's marathon were acheived between 2000 and 2009. The advances in training, injury prevention, footwear and technology should all make it easier for current runners to outperform their predecessors. So why isn't it happening in Britain?

There was a time, long ago, when intelligent people believed the earth was fl at, and the best treatment for every disease was to have leeches drink your blood. Nowadays we know so much better and we laugh at their foolish naivety. I suspect, however, that in years to come people will look back at us with equal astonishment. Anthropologists of the future will roll their eyes to the sky, and with jaws agape and arms akimbo, they will ask in utter bewilderment how people of our time were intelligent enough to have a world wide web of information, satellite communications, laser technology, transplant surgery, and at the same time thought it was a good idea to have non-competitive sports day in our schools.

They will be amazed that despite all our advances in medical science, we had so completely lost touch with our own bodies that we suffered in our millions from obesity, diabetes and heart disease. Th ey will probably condemn as criminals the politicians who sold school playing fields for housing. They will be unable to understand how these people could justify the pittance they received for the land, with the enormous cost to the health service of treating the increasing levels of obesity, diabetes and heart disease, that their actions helped to bring about.

In October 1998 the Education and Standards Framework Act was passed, and Section 77 stated that every decision on the disposal of a school playing field had to be taken by the Education Secretary. Before this, it was estimated that more than 5,000 playing fields had been sold off, with most of them going to property developers. Between October 1998 and September 2001, the Education Secretary looked at 167 cases, and gave consent for 161. Only six were refused, which suggests that the sale of school fields is government policy. How can children get the physical activity that is essential for their development if they have nowhere to exercise?

I have tried to understand the arguments for non-competitive sports day, but they don't make any sense. Every single aspect of life is competitive and to deny this, and hide children from it, is irresponsible. They say that the children who come last at sports day shouldn't be subjected to such public humiliation. I've been to a lot of sports events and school sports, and I have never seen anybody laughed at or humiliated for trying their best.

I know I shouldn't use myself as a solitary example to make a point, but I'm going to anyway. I came last in my first school sports day race, and I felt bad about it. It didn't make me hate sport; it made me determined to do better next time. The reasons I did better next time were twofold: I found an event which suited me better, and I did a lot of exercise and practice. It is also worth mentioning again that I was in a class of 42, and there was a chart on the classroom wall with all our names in descending order of academic performance. Throughout that year I was reminded every day that there were at least 40 children in that class doing better than me, but despite my apparent failures, I now have a professional degree and my own business.

The reason I have done this is attitude – attitude to failure.

There is an American, who rejoices in the name of Zig Zigler, who coined the phrase 'Failure is an event, not a person.' It means that failing at something does not brand you as a failure; it simply means that on this occasion you failed. He likes to tell the story of Thomas Edison who was trying to invent an electric light, but had failed to do so after 5,000 attempts. A reporter went to see him and asked why he continued with such a pointless task after 5,000 failures. Edison replied that he hadn't failed at all because he had successfully eliminated 5,000 ways that did not work, which meant he was 5,000 steps closer to finding the way that would work. Realising that you have failed at something gives you the opportunity to improve, and do better next time. Becoming better at something, as time goes by, is enormously enjoyable and life-enhancing. It builds self confidence and esteem. Why would people in education want to deny children the opportunity to fail at something and then to improve? If they are unable to explain to children that 'failure is an event, not a person' they shouldn't be involved in education.

Having said all that, I think school sport has to improve a great deal. Not everybody is suited to competitive ball games, and physical education at school should offer something for everybody. To make school sport all-inclusive, I would like to see groups of schools employing peripatetic PE specialists. Instead of each school employing one PE teacher, four schools could employ four teachers who would travel between the schools on a co-ordinated timetable, and offer sufficient diversity to engage every child in enjoyable sport.

When every child enjoys regular, strenuous physical activity their health will improve, and the spread of obesity will be curtailed. A less obvious but equally important consequence would be an improvement in academic standards. It is 2,000 years since the Roman poet Juvenal, wrote about the importance of a healthy mind in a healthy body (*mens sana in corpore sano*), and recent discoveries in the world of neuroscience have proved why he was correct.

Brain chemistry is enormously complicated, and what follows is enormously simplified, but in essence there is a substance in the brain called brain derived neurotrophic factor (BDNF), which allows brain cells to grow and make connections with other cells. Learning something new involves making new nerve cell connections in the brain. Recent experiments have shown that levels of BDNF are significantly increased by exercise, and therefore learning is enhanced by the chemical effects of exercise.

This surely means that exercise should be the cornerstone of every school day, rather than an occasional extra activity. If you are not convinced, consider this: BDNF, along with other exercise-induced regulators, plays a significant part in insulin sensitivity and cellular metabolism. When those two things malfunction, you get diabetes and obesity. This is oversimplified again, but a person without sufficient exercise becomes like a hibernating animal, except that a hibernating animal doesn't keep eating. Reducing calorie intake is not enough to prevent weight gain in someone whose metabolism malfunctions because of a lack of exercise-induced regulators. We evolved to be energetic, so why don't we encourage our children to be energetic every day?

Of course, teachers and politicians are not solely to blame. Parents have to allow and encourage children to have energetic outdoor activity. Every hour spent in front of a television or computer screen, instead of exercising, is an hour's contribution to the child's future ill-health. Coaches from various sports now often complain that young people are not as fit, healthy and tough as they used to be.

It may appear that I have digressed from the falling

standards of distance runners, but a high level of general fitness among younger people, leads to larger numbers becoming involved in serious sport. Within a large number there will always be several with real talent. Standards are falling in distance running because the number of young, competitive runners is falling, and that is happening for several reasons, only one of which is the lack of general fitness.

The image of distance running has changed considerably over the last thirty years. The sport has a much higher profile now thanks to events like the London Marathon and Great North Run, but I wonder if those events have ruined the sport's image in the eyes of young people. I was introduced to running at school, but I got excited about it at local road races, when I saw how fast men could run for mile after mile. These guys were fit and lean and tough. They would compete as hard as they could, and then chat and joke with each other straight after. I would go back to school after the weekend and my friends were impressed that I had been running at the same event as Jim Alder and other top runners in the area.

Nowadays, children who like running at school are presented with events on television which are full of people who can't run very well, or wearing silly costumes. When they tell their friends they were at a local race at the weekend, the response is likely to be, 'Oh yeah, my mother did that with some of her friends because they are all trying to lose weight.' It's a long time since I was young, but I can't imagine a teenager thinks that sounds very cool.

Road racing used to be a serious sport for competitive runners, but it has been high-jacked by charities and over-weight joggers. I think it's great that people of all ages and abilities are trying to exercise and get fit, but I am concerned that the image of road running in a teenager's mind has changed from the attractive one I had, to something they would dread. What teenager would long to do the same activity that their mother and father do badly?

Of course, serious athletes still compete in local events, but those events are much harder to see. When I started running, road racing events were held on Saturday afternoon on the road, and people were quite likely to come across them by chance. As the roads got busier, the races were all moved to Sunday morning. Eventually, the police changed their attitude, and forced most road races off the road into parks, or into cross country events, because people on their way to Sunday shopping were being inconvenienced.

For example, the Morpeth to Newcastle Road Race was held on New Year's Day, and it was England's oldest annual road race having begun in 1902. By its very nature, it couldn't be moved, so in 2006 it was forced out of existence by the police and local authorities, who required a payment of £30,000, to ensure that all safety requirements were met. A local road race can't possibly afford that sort of money. Of course safety is paramount, but when an historic, local event is killed off by the people entrusted with protecting and serving our local communities, I think something has gone badly wrong.

Running is losing an influx of talent to the enormous popularity of football. The fame and fortune enjoyed by Premier League players is so extraordinary that vast numbers of youngsters want to emulate their heroes. Local football leagues are thriving, which at least means that plenty of young people are enjoying exercise through competitive sport, but it also means that competition for places is becoming much greater. In contrast, the reduced numbers in Athletics mean that competition for places has declined. The paradox is that it has never been harder for a British born footballer to play for a top class club, while it has never been easier for a distance runner to make the British Olympic team.

With so much money involved in football, lots of people want to get their share and football managers have started complaining about the tactics of players' agents. I believe that running has been badly damaged by certain agents, who are nothing more than parasites upon the sport. The sort of road race, in which I was winning a television set many years ago, may now offer a first prize of up to £1,000. Agents, with a string of good African runners, will bring someone in to all of these races and take their percentage of the winnings. This is bad news for everybody except the agent and his runner. The local runners, who are making sacrifices to be their best, are denied the chance to win some money that might make a real difference to them. If the race was won by a local runner, instead of a foreigner nobody has heard of, it would generate much more local publicity, which would be good for the event, the sponsor and the sport. Local runners, who are trying to break through to the next level, need to learn how to win races. Learning how to make the move that wins a race is an essential part of developing into a better runner. Being thrashed out of sight, by somebody who is just too good, is simply demoralising. I would stop this problem by having British only prize money in this type of race.

It is usually thought that money and professionalism go hand in hand, but it isn't always so. My contemporaries from the 1980s, who still dominate the British ranking lists, were amateur sportsmen because they all had jobs to earn their living. Their attitude and dedication to running, however, was entirely professional. There appears to be an attitude now that a top class runner has to be a full time runner, and therefore has to be professional, in the sense of making money from it. The problem is that you have to be very good to make a decent living from it, and lots of professional runners are struggling to make enough to get by. The irony here is that amateur runners in the past would go training after work and dream of heroic deeds, while the professional runners of today can train in the afternoon but worry how to pay the gas bill.

When the National Lottery started in the mid '90s, it was assumed that sport would benefit hugely from lottery funding. It has clearly worked for cycling but not for distance running. Cycling has succeeded because of the vision and organisation which athletics has lacked. Cycling used its lottery money to create a centre of excellence to which the best riders were invited. Th e chosen ones were given everything they needed to perform. Accommodation, facilities, equipment, coaching, physiotherapy and psychology were all provided in an atmosphere of excellence, but you were either in or you were out. You did it the official way, or not at all.

Runners deemed good enough to receive lottery funding have simply been sent a cheque to help them out. It seems to me that this makes lottery funding become the goal for many runners. Suddenly, you don't have to worry about the bills, and you can enjoy your *professional runner* lifestyle, without anybody insisting that you become the greatest you can be. I think athletics has to adopt the cycling approach for its middle and long distance runners.

Another big problem which damages the image of running is cheating. Taking drugs to enhance performance is wrong on all counts; it is morally wrong; it is against the rules; it is potentially dangerous; and drug cheats leave their sport in a worse condition than when they joined it, which is an act of despicable selfishness. I don't think anybody sets out to be a drug cheat when they join the sport. I think most of them reach a point where they find it hard to improve and decide that a few tablets or injections will bring the success they crave. They, or the coaches who initiate it, fail to understand the consequences of what they are doing. They lack the intelligence, or the morality, to see the bigger picture.

Erythropoietin (EPO) is used by endurance athletes to increase the production of red blood cells, and therefore increase the transport of oxygen to working muscles. In the late 80's several young cyclists on EPO died in their sleep because their blood had become too viscous to flow properly, and EPO cheats now take an anti-coagulant with their drug to stay alive. The use of anabolic steroids to increase muscular strength has a wide variety of possible effects, depending on the dose and steroid used. Putting an exogenous steroid into the body alters the balance of naturally occurring hormones, and this can lead to raised cholesterol, acne, sterility in males and females, masculine features in women, breast development in men, stunted growth in children and psychological changes which are often referred to as 'roid rage'.

I have always believed that the point of competitive sport was to see how good you could become, and then take enormous satisfaction and contentment from whatever success you managed to achieve. The people who take performance enhancing drugs must have a different attitude to mine, because I don't understand how much satisfaction you get from a career based upon your choice of pharmaceuticals. I guess it isn't satisfaction they want: it is glory, fame and fortune. These people must think that sport is all about seeing what you can get out of it, but they are wrong, because sport is all about seeing what it gets out of you.

I have previously espoused the benefits of thinking differently to most people. The trouble with thinking differently is that you can end up with ideas that almost nobody else shares, and this may well be one of them. I have a theory about one of the most famous cheats of all time. I reckon that most cheats think they are only cheating if they get caught, and the best example of this is Diego Maradona in the quarter finals of the 1986 World Cup. Argentina beat England 2-1, and I am sure everybody knows that Maradona scored the first goal with his hand. The referee and linesman didn't see it, and gave the goal. Maradona knew he had scored with his hand but kept quiet, because he thought he had got away with it. However, photographers and television both had indisputable evidence.

Argentina went on to win the World Cup and Maradona was regarded as the greatest player in the world. Soon afterwards Maradona started to have problems with over indulgence in food, drink and drugs, and he continued to have those problems for many years. He was banned from football for 15 months in 1991 for taking cocaine, and he was sent home from the 1994 World Cup for taking the stimulant ephedrine.

The handball goal is a fact, and his drug taking disgrace is a fact. My theory simply puts them together. He was the best player in the world but he cheated to win the World Cup. Imagine if he had gone to the referee and said 'That's a free kick to England because it hit my hand.' Imagine if Argentina had still gone on to win. He would have been the best player in the world and a great sportsman. He would have been a shining example to every sportsman everywhere. When he left football, it would have been a greater sport because of him. But he didn't, and my theory is that those very ideas plagued him, and bothered him so much that he turned to over-indulgence and drugs, and his career and life went downhill.

I have no idea what books he reads but I am going to guess that Diego Maradona has never read Fyodor Dostoevsky's *Crime and Punishment*. If you haven't read it yet I won't spoil it for you, but I will recommend that anyone contemplating cheating should read it before they do so. It might save them from a great deal of anguish, and the slippery slope that lead to Maradona's banishment from the sport he once graced.

Success in running, and most other things, comes down to attitude. Cheating or not cheating is down to attitude. My reason for running was to see if I could do it, and I was trying to impress myself. I think most cheats cheat because they want to impress everybody else. The end is more important than the means, and they want to be seen to be the winner. In our modern, brash, conspicuous society we have become extremely extrovert, and behaviour that would have been scandalous years ago is now seen as normal. Extroverts are seen as happy, cheerful, sociable, fun-loving people, and introverts are regarded as quiet, boring, dull people. These are the popular stereotypes, but they are not an accurate definition of the two types.

A better definition would be this: an extrovert thinks outwardly, and an introvert thinks inwardly. An extrovert cares more about how other people see them. Introverts care more about how they see themselves. Extroverts depend on other people's opinion for a stimulus to their actions. Introverts depend on their internal sense of right and wrong to make their way in the world. Extroverts look on the faces of others to gauge themselves, while introverts look in the mirror. Let me tell you that I am an introvert, and I am going to shout it from the rooftops.

CHAPTER 14

BE CAREFUL WHAT YOU DREAM

Throughout my running career, my wildest dream was to win an Olympic medal. It was a very wild dream, because I took running seriously from the age of 16 and I was 32 before I even made it to the Olympic team. I had lots of specific goals along the way, but in the back of my mind an Olympic medal was always the ultimate achievement. The performance I produced in Los Angeles still gives me a profound sense of satisfaction. I ran the very best race I could because I trained extremely well, and I had my mind completely focused. The context was everything. I ran the race of my life because it was the biggest race of my life. This Olympic marathon gave me the opportunity to fulfil my wildest dream.

Context is everything, and this may seem like splitting hairs, but I have often thought about it since. When I ran round the track in the Coliseum just behind John Treacy, I was trying as hard as I could to beat him and get a silver medal. But those thoughts of silver being better than bronze were just thoughts. On a superficial level I was trying as hard as I could, but deep down I was doing cartwheels of joy because I was fulfilling my lifelong dream.

I can explain this better if I can get you to come with me on one of my journeys of imagination. I used to pretend that I had a team of people inside me, and each one was responsible for part of the system, like the heart, or lungs, or legs, or energy production. There was a foreman who kept them all working hard and passed on my requirements. Try to imagine the scene as we enter the Olympic stadium in third place having worked flat out for over two hours.

'Come on, lads, he wants more effort,' says the foreman.

'What for?' ask the lads.

'He says he wants a silver medal, and it's just a couple of yards in front of us.'

'What do you mean he wants a silver medal? He has never once mentioned a silver medal before. It's always just been a medal, and bronze is a medal. We've been flogging our guts out for 16 years to get him a medal, and now that he's one minute away from achieving it he's changed his mind! I don't think so.'

It may seem obvious that second is better than third, but finding more effort when you are already exhausted requires more than a logical idea. I ran that lap of the track as fast as I could, within the context of my lifelong dreams. If Treacy and I had been racing for first place, or for third and fourth, I think I would have been able to find more effort, because the outcome would have mattered considerably more than the difference between silver and bronze. If my dream had always been to win gold or silver, I would have been able to run faster in that last half mile. I am not saying that I would have beaten him because he may well have found more too. I just think it's interesting that I had a long term goal, which for most of my career was ridiculously ambitious, but in the last few minutes it wasn't high enough.

They say you should be careful what you dream because it might come true, but you should also be careful what you promise. After finishing sixth in Seoul with poor preparation, I started to think that I could still run well for a year or two, and shortly after getting home from Korea I was asked to run the London Marathon again. They had a new sponsor in TDK, and had appointed David Bedford to assemble a field which would make London the best city marathon in the world. He offered me an appearance fee which was vastly more than I had ever had before. I accepted. I felt it was time I started to get some financial reward for all my years of effort.

I trained through the winter and into the spring with a mixture of success and problems. When the race got close, I knew I wasn't really running well enough to do myself justice. I was going alright but it wasn't good enough to compete with the best. I could have run with the leaders to halfway, then feigned an injury and dropped out. I would have gone home with a princely sum of money, but it would have felt like mugging my grandmother. The marathon had provided me with the greatest moments of my life, and I felt a duty to provide it with performances to be proud of. I wanted my record at the marathon to be the best it could be, and I would never swap my honour for money.

Nowadays top class sportsmen can make an extraordinary fortune, and to put my 'princely sum' into context, it was about what an average Premiership footballer makes in a week. I don't have a problem with people making lots of money, as long as they act in a way which is good for their sport. I don't like it when they forget why they are paid so much.

I am talking about the people who think they deserve a fortune because they are so good at what they do. In my view, that's not why they are paid so much. They are paid a fortune because their sport is so popular. Sport goes on through the years and decades, and performers have their brief moment in the limelight until someone else has their turn. All the wealthy sports have a fabulous history of sublime moments, tenacious underdogs, and all-conquering heroes, and this rich history makes people want to watch in their millions. Today's stars are paid so much thanks to the great achievements of the people who went before them. Therefore, whilst in the limelight, it is their duty to maintain the honour and integrity of their sport, so when they pass it on to the next generation it is better than, or at least as good as, when they arrived.

I have no problem with great sportsmen making a fortune, but I have a big problem with people who think their fame and fortune make them more important than the sport itself; who think they should win at any cost; and who think cheating is just something to get away with.

Integrity, I am pleased to say, can still be found. I pulled out of London a week before the race, but Dave Bedford paid me a quarter of the appearance fee for my honesty, and a promise that I would run next year for the same deal. I carried on training because I had secured a deal for almost as much money to run an autumn marathon in Beijing. For different reasons this was another marathon I didn't run.

This was 1989, and on June 4th about 200 people were killed in pro-democracy protests in Tiananmen Square, precisely where the marathon was due to start. This was another matter of honour; I couldn't go to China and run across the blood stained streets just for money. I pulled out. I think individuals are entitled to boycott sporting events for their beliefs, but, at the same time, I disagree with countries forcing their individuals to boycott for political reasons.

In 1980, America boycotted the Moscow Olympics because Russia had invaded Afghanistan. Margaret Thatcher wanted Britain to follow suit, but she couldn't force the team to stay away. The irony of political interference in sport is no better demonstrated than by the fact that all these years later the Russians are gone and Afghanistan is now occupied by armies from both America and Britain.

My first two chances to earn good money had gone astray, but I entered 1990 with high hopes of a good performance in London, and that big appearance fee. I was in my late thirties by now, and although I was still capable of running really well, I was taking longer to get over injuries and niggles. I had several setbacks which meant that I had to withdraw from London again.

At the end of the year, I went to Japan to run the famous Fukuoka marathon. I was doing alright in the second group when I pulled a calf muscle just after halfway. I stopped and then limped for a while, but I realised that I couldn't limp 12 miles back to the finish, so I ended my marathon running career sitting on the kerb in a Japanese street, waiting for the drop-out bus to pick me up.

Be careful what you promise because a pact is binding. My utter determination to be 6th rather than 7th in Seoul made me promise to myself that I would never run another marathon, and despite the opportunity for four very large paydays, I never did. You might think it was just a combination of circumstances and my age that prevented me from finishing any of those four marathons, but I am not so sure. In Los Angeles I made a pact with myself that I was going to run the best race of my life and I did. To reach the finish in one piece in Seoul, I made a pact with myself, and did it. When you make a pact that involves such extremes of effort and commitment, you surely have to take the consequences, as well as the benefits. I believe that my Olympic medal was won not through physical ability but by utter commitment to the Olympic ideal. That level of commitment, even when there was no medal to be won, led me to make a promise that eventually cost me a lot of money. But I would not have had it any other way, because I would never have been offered the money without the medal, and I would never have won the medal without the commitment.

If I had to choose between the medal and the money, I would always choose the medal. Even if you have stacks of money there will always be people with lots more than you, but with an Olympic medal you can name all the people who have one. And no matter how much money you have you can't buy a medal, though having said that, I won't refuse if anybody wants to make a ridiculously large offer for mine. But after parting with your money, you would then be the proud owner of my medal. You would own it, but it would always be my medal.

It was always the really big races that motivated me most. It was always at the top events that my inner caterpillar turned into a butterfly. I ran all my best races when I was able to peak both physically and mentally. When I peaked successfully I knew I would beat people who might normally beat me. The ability to peak correctly gives runners like me the chance to step up from our normal level to something much greater. I peaked so well for Los Angeles that I felt confident that I could beat people like Seko and de Castella. Peaking correctly gives outsiders their greatest chance of success, but it can only take you so far.

Los Angeles and London '85 were perhaps my two best races. In the last few miles of each event, I raced shoulder to shoulder with Treacy and then Jones. I knew I had peaked and that I was running a world class performance. In each race I believed that I could beat my opponent, but in each race they beat me. I have spoken to each of them since and I am sure the reason is the same. I *thought* I could beat them, but they *knew* they could beat me. They knew they could beat me because they had done it many times before. Peaking is a fantastic way for an underdog to shine, but it is always better if you can be consistently top class.

Peaking for the big events allowed me to be successful as I defined success in Chapter 6. 'Success is measured by how much I fulfil the talent I was born with.' Making the most of who you are is a triumph of Olympic proportions that is available to everybody who tries. It is a concept that is embedded in the Olympic Creed. Unfortunately the Olympic Creed is nearly always misquoted.

You often hear people say, 'It's not the winning that counts; it's the taking part.' I really don't like to hear that because it implies that winning doesn't matter, just turn up and enjoy it. It is a dreadful misquote. It is a misquote by omission and it fails to explain 'taking part'. The complete Olympic Creed explains it fully:

'The most important thing in the Olympic Games is not to win but to take part, just as the most important thing in life is not the triumph but the struggle. The essential thing is not to have conquered but to have fought well.'

Throughout this book I have related many of my struggles, because overcoming adversity usually makes a more interesting story. I have failed to mention the hundreds of entries in my training diaries which, apart from detailing my daily workouts, also highlight how I felt. As I have reread these entries, I have been struck by how many have comments like 'felt good', 'moving well', 'beautiful day', 'felt great', 'felt easy', 'enjoyed it', 'loved it'. Looking again at my diaries has reminded me how much pleasure I got from the daily involvement in my sport, and how lucky I was to have discovered and revelled in the sheer, innate joy of running. Of course, all the enjoyable running was directed towards competition and it is in competition that all my running should be judged. I ran some good races and some bad ones, but I am left with a deep contentment because I got close to the limit that my talent would allow.

When I have discussed my career at runners' seminars, I have often been asked to name my greatest moment, but the question would usually include a choice between winning the London Marathon and being third in the Olympics. Both of these are very high on my list, but neither one is my greatest moment. My reply would often cause surprise because my greatest moment was not a result, but a spell of running which lasted about five minutes.

The greatest moment in my two decades of running came 22 miles into the Olympic marathon when I took the lead and pushed the pace. After all my setbacks, injuries and failures, I was living the fantasy that every distance runner has on a long, cold winter run. I had the initiative, I was calling the tune. I was grasping my opportunity with both hands. I was taking part in Olympic proportions. I was running as fast as I dared. I was trying my utmost to fulfil my wildest dreams. Today was indeed the day. I was doing it. I was flying and I felt absolutely fantastic.

APPENDIX

The following is an exact copy of my training diary from the London marathon to the Olympic marathon. After each week I have added comments to explain my reasoning.

May 13th	London Marathon	1st in 2:09:57
Mon 14th	too stiff to run	
Tues 15th	rest	
Wed 16th	4 miles easy run	
Thur 17th	5 miles steady run	
Frid 18th	5 miles steady run	
Sat 20th	6 miles steady run	
Sun 21st	10 miles in 65 minutes	

I ran only thirty miles this week because I was mentally drained and my legs were very sore. Steady running for me was about 6 minutes per mile, and an easy run was 7 minutes per mile or slower.

Mon 21st	7 miles steady run
Tues 22nd	9 miles steady run
Wed 23rd	7 miles steady run
Thur 24th	5 miles steady run
Fri 25th	am. 5 miles steady
	pm. 6 miles easy
Sat 26th	7 miles including 12 x 100 yard strides with 100 jog, to stretch legs
Sun 27th	10 miles steady.

I was in no hurry to rush back into training and only felt fully recovered after 56 miles of steady running. The real benefit of taking two weeks to recover was clear in how eager I felt to start training again.

Mon 28th	15 miles in 90 minutes
Tues 29th	am. 7 miles steady
	pm. Track - 6 x 1000m (with 2m 30s jog)
	2 min 57 sec, 2:57, 2:55, 2:55, 2:52, 2:52
Wed 30th	am. 8 miles steady run
	pm 5 miles steady
Thur 31st	15 miles in 90 mins
Fri 1st June	am. 7 miles steady
	pm. 5 miles steady
Sat 2nd	Race - Northern 5,000 metres . 11th in 14:30
Sun 3rd	15 miles easy - felt tired

I wasn't sure how I would go in my first track session, so I ran the first two kilometre reps conservatively. I ran the next pair a little quicker, and because I felt good, I ran the last two quicker still. I didn't want to start too fast and be forced to slow down, because that is bad for self confidence. The race was a poor performance, but a decent training session. I increased my miles for the week to 91.

Mon 4th	am. 7 miles steady
	pm. 5 miles steady
Tues 5th	am. 7 miles steady
	pm. Track - 10 x 400m (90 sec jog) av. 64.2 sec
Wed 6th	am. 7 miles steady
	pm. 7 miles steady
Thur 7th	15 miles in 89 mins
Fri 8th	am. 7 miles steady

	pm. 5 miles steady
Sat 9th	am. 5 miles steady
	pm. Race - Blaydon Races - 3rd to Kevin
	Forster in 25.50 (5.6 miles)
Sun 10th	20 miles steady

This week shows the typical structure of my marathon training. Two long runs; a 20 miler feeling comfortable to build endurance, and a 15 mile run at a brisk pace without straining. Two speed sessions; a track session of 400 metre reps may seem short for a marathon runner, but I needed to work on speed all the time. Even a marathon is a race won by the fastest runner. The other speed session could be another track session or a race or a hill session. Monday, Wednesday and Friday were always steady running to recover from the faster work. My volume of running was up to 101 miles for the week.

Mon 11th	am. 6 miles steady
	pm. 8 miles steady
Tues 12th	am. 7 miles steady
	pm. Track - 16 x 200m (200m jog) av 31.4 sec
Wed 13th	am. 7 miles steady
	pm. 7 miles steady
Thur 14th	15 miles in 86 mins
Fri 15th	am. 5 miles steady
	pm. 7 miles steady
Sat 16th	am. Track - 5 x 1600m in 4 min 40 sec with
	400m float in 90 sec.
	pm. 4 miles easy
Sun 17th	20 miles steady

The Saturday track session was one of my benchmarks. It was basically 10,000 meters of continuous running made up of four laps in 70 seconds, then a lap in 90 seconds, with the whole sequence repeated five times. It adds up to 31 minutes for 10K. There are no rest periods during a marathon, and this session trained me to recover from mile efforts while running at six minute per mile pace. 103 miles for the week.

Mon 18th	am. 9 miles steady
	pm. 5 miles steady
Tues 19th	am. 5 miles steady
	pm. Track- 3 x 800m in 2 min 9.5 sec (2 min rec.) I was supposed to run 6 x 800 but my calves were getting a little tight so I changed the rest of it to 2 x 400m in 64 and 5 x 100m strides
Wed 20th	am. 8 miles steady
	pm. 7 miles steady
Thur 21st	15 miles in 91 mins
Fri 22nd	am. 6 miles steady
	pm. drove 4 hours to London
Sat 23rd	am. 2 miles easy
	pm. AAA 10,000m. Dropped out 5K (14:35); ran 5 miles in the evening
Sun 24th	15 miles steady - drove 4 hours home

This was a bad week. My calf muscles were tight from the build-up in my training. I ran the AAA 10K because I was defending champion, but I wasn't in shape to run a track race at that level, and I wasn't motivated enough either. It was a mistake to run the race, but I knew my mind was on Los Angeles, and I wasn't too worried. 89 miles for the week.

Mon 25th	am. 6 miles steady
	pm. 9 miles steady

Tues 26th	am. 6 miles steady
	pm. Track - 5 miles on the road in 25 minutes, then 800, 1000, 800, 1000, 800 (all with 2 mins rec.) in 2:18, 2:51, 2:18, 2:52, 2:16
Wed 27th	am. 6 miles steady
	pm. 8 miles steady
Thur 28th	20 miles steady
Fri 29th	am. 7 miles steady
	Flew to Boston for heat acclimatisation
Sat 30th	am. 9 miles steady
	pm 6 miles with 20 mins of 15 sec stride/15 jog
Sun 1st July	15 miles steady (75 F and 80% humidity)

The track session was designed to work on pace, with the tiredness of 5 miles fast running in my legs. I swapped the 20 miler to Thursday because I was travelling the next day. Saturday's session was done with a running watch. Every time the watch hit a minute or 30 seconds I strode hard for 15 seconds, leaving me 15 seconds to recover before I went again. This gave me a high heart rate for 20 minutes, and worked on my speed. I couldn't do both things for twenty minutes using the long repetitions of marathon training.

Spending the last six weeks in the heat and humidity of Boston was essential if I was going to cope with the weather in Los Angeles. 102 miles for the week.

Mon 2nd	am. 6 miles steady - hamstring pulling
	pm. rest and treatment
Tues 3rd	am. flew to Atlanta
	pm. 7 miles steady - leg ok
Wed 4th	8 am. Peachtree 10K road race - 11th in 29:30
	pm. 5 miles easy then flew to Boston
Thurs 5th	16 miles steady (85 F and 85% humidity)

Fri 6th	am. 6 miles steady
	pm. 2 miles easy, 1 mile hard effort, 1 mile steady, 10 x 600m Pump House hill, 2 miles easy
Sat 7th	am. 6 miles steady
	pm. 9 miles - felt good
Sun 8th	21 miles interval session on the road. Timed efforts of these minutes 5, 1, 2, 4, 1, 2, 5, 1, 2, 4, 1, 2, 5, all with 5 mins steady running between; 10 mins steady at start and finish, no jogging at any stage. Very tiring, I had to lie down for 2 hours afterwards.

This was a big week, despite covering only 92 miles. A 10k race, and a tough hill session set me up for the hardest session I ever ran. Sunday's session was the perfect session to prepare me to race a marathon rather than to run it. Using a continuous watch I ran steady for 10 minutes, ran hard for 5 minutes, then steady for 5 minutes. The next effort was 1 minute, then 2 minutes, then 4 minutes, with 5 minutes steady in between every effort. I repeated the sequence except the third effort was 5 minutes instead of four. I repeated both sequences again. This session teaches total concentration, pace judgement, and the essential ability to surge and surge again on demand as you get more tired. I used different periods of effort so I could go with someone else's surge in a race, when I didn't know how long the surge was going to last. This is not a session to get you fit, you have to be fit to contemplate it. It is the session, which I believe, changed me from a marathon runner to a marathon racer.

Mon 9th	am. 6 miles easy
	pm. 10 miles easy
Tues 10th	am. 6 miles steady

	pm. 8 miles steady
Wed 11th	am. 6 miles steady
	pm. Track - 2 x (2 x 800, 1 x 1600), 2 x 800
	all with 2 min 30 jog
	2:15, 2:14, 4:29, 2:13, 2:15, 4:28, 2:15, 2:11
Thur 12th	15 miles in 88 mins
Fri 13th	am. 5 miles steady
	pm. 7 miles steady
Sat 14th	4.8 mile road race 1st in 22:49
	pm. 8 miles steady
Sun 15th	20 miles steady (85 F, 85% humidity)

I needed two days of steady running before I felt recovered from last Sunday. The significant part of the track session was trying to run the miles at the same pace as I ran the half miles. It was nice to win a road race. 107 miles for the week.

Mon 16th	am. 6 miles steady
	pm. 8 miles steady
Tues 17th	am. 6 miles steady
	pm. Track - 600 in 93.3, 45 sec jog, 1200 in
	3:34, 100 sec jog, 4 x 200 in 30 with 20 sec
	turn around, 45 sec jog, 1600 in 4:50, 2 min
	jog, 800 in 2:05.9 (sprint and coast alternate
	50m), 45 sec jog, 1600 in 4:48
Wed 18th	15 miles in 90 mins - tired.
Thur 19th	am. 7 miles steady
	pm. 8 miles easy
Fri 20th	am. 7 miles steady
	pm. Track - 2 sets of 8 x 200 with 20 sec jog.
	Av 30 sec.
Sat 21st	am. 6 miles steady
	pm. 7 miles steady
Sun 22nd	Race 8 miles: 3rd in 39:22 Felt flat.

Tuesday's track session looks complicated, but it was all about running something fast and recovering at slightly quicker than marathon pace. Friday's session is one I used to do as a 5,000 meter runner, and fast reps with short recoveries have always helped me to peak. The marathon was getting close and I wanted to be as sharp as possible. I ran poorly in the race because I couldn't commit myself fully. My sub-conscious was saving everything for the one that mattered, and I knew from past experience that deep in my mind I was still a caterpillar waiting for the right day to transform. 98 miles for the week.

Mon 23rd	am. 6 miles steady
	pm. 7 miles steady
Tues 24th	28 miles in 2:55 (85 F and humid - lost 9lbs in fluid) felt strong
Wed 25th	am. 6 miles steady
	pm. 7 miles steady
Thur 26th	am. 7 miles steady
	pm. 7 miles steady
Fri 27th	am. 5 miles steady
	pm. Track - 10 x 400 with 90 sec jog, av 62 sec
Sat 28th	8 miles easy
Sun 29th	18 miles interval session in 1:43. timed efforts of (mins) 4,1,2,4,1,2,4,1,2,4,1,2 all with 5 mins steady between, 10 min steady start and finish

I think it is important to run further than the marathon on one occasion about three weeks prior. I gave myself two days of steady running to recover before doing another speed track session. I finished my intense training with another interval session, but reduced it slightly because I knew I was in good shape and didn't want to over train. 104 miles for the week.

Mon 30th	am. 6 miles steady
	pm. 6 miles steady
Tues 31st	am. 9 miles steady
	pm. 5 miles steady
Wed 1st Aug	am. 6 miles steady
	pm. Track - 6 x 800 in 2:10 with 2:30 jog in 91 F, 85% hum.
Thur 2nd	am. 5 miles steady
	pm. 5 miles steady
Fri 3rd	15 miles in 96 mins (85 F) felt good
Sat 4th	am. 5 miles easy
	pm. 5 miles steady
Sun 5th	Race - 5 miles 1st in 24:09 Felt strong

I reduced the mileage to 84. I felt sharp in my track session, and very fluent when winning a 5 mile race. I was getting nervous, but knew I had trained well.

Mon 6th	am. 9 miles Flew Boston to Los Angeles
Tues 7th	6 miles steady
Wed 8th	am. 6 miles steady
	pm. Track - 5 x 400 with lap jog av 60.9
Thur 9th	5 miles steady
Fri 10th	5 miles steady
Sat 11th	rest
Sun 12th	Olympic Marathon - 3rd in 2:09:58